Remo Bufano's BOOK OF PUPPETRY

Remo Bufano's
BOOK OF
PUPPETRY

EDITED AND COMPILED
BY
ARTHUR RICHMOND

✦

Drawings by Remo Bufano

THE MACMILLAN COMPANY
New York

CONTENTS

PREFACE

─<✵>─

FOR ALMOST THIRTY YEARS in America the name Remo Bufano was synonymous with marionettes. The theatre, motion pictures, radio, and television were gayer and more colorful for his highly original work. Countless children and adults thrilled to his saucy creations and went away happier from his plays.

Over the course of those busy and fruitful years he occasionally took time out to tell of his magic art. There was the successful *Be a Puppet Showman* and several books of plays especially written for the marionette theatre. Unfortunately these books went out of print and are difficult to obtain. To meet the needs of all those who have sought them and for the new, ever-growing band of puppet enthusiasts, the publishers have made available again all the material contained in those helpful volumes.

Here are practical, easy-to-follow directions on all phases of puppetry. There are also included some new methods of construction and advice on new materials, for Remo, up to the day of his tragic death, was busy experimenting with new mediums.

This book is dedicated to all those who shared his enthusiasm. If you have a love for the magic world of make-believe, there is no better or more fascinating path to follow than to the land of marionettes. So step right this way and let this book be your passport. Bring along a great deal of enthusiasm, a fair share of patience, and a little mechanical and artistic common sense.

But before you sharpen your tools and mix your paint and measure your cloth, let us take a quick glance at the marionette's past.

ARTHUR RICHMOND

Remo Bufano's BOOK OF PUPPETRY

THE PUPPET'S TALE

-<✵>-

A SHORT HISTORY OF PUPPETRY

MARIONETTES are of the world of magic. They are mighty little magicians who have exerted a power and enchanted the hearts of kings and queens, rich and poor, sages and fools. They have performed their antics on street corners, in palaces, theatres, churches, in splendid cities and simple villages.

It is very plain that they have a history—and a very fascinating one. According to fragments of scattered evidence marionettes seem to have existed since the beginning of the world. Originally they were not like marionettes as we understand them today. The development must have been very slow and probably accidental.

The first marionettes were not used as entertainment, but as figures in religious ceremonies. There is sufficient reason to believe that the birth of the marionette came about in the church, like the theatre itself.

The very name marionette was inspired by little statues of the Virgin Mary sometime during the Middle Ages. Some of the marionettes were extremely beautiful in design and oddly enough people constantly compared them to the little statues of Mary in their homes until the name marionette (little Mary) came to mean only one thing.

But long before this marionettes existed in ancient lands. It is possible that the first marionettes, like the first of so many other things, originally made their appearance in China.

1

We know that they were used in ancient Egypt, Rome, and Greece. It is interesting to note that the Sanskrit equivalent of stage manager, Sutrad Hara, literally means "thread holder."

Dolls, as you all know, are as old as man, and it is highly probable that the first marionettes were dolls to which imaginative fathers added movable limbs to amuse their children. Terra cotta dolls, with movable arms and legs, have been found in ancient tombs all over the world.

Some authorities believe that the ancient idols were the beginning of marionettes. Thousands of years ago clever mechanics made huge figures that moved as if by a miracle. The working mechanism was so carefully thought out that the idols could be made to raise and lower their arms, raise and turn their massive heads and even open and close their eyes.

Movable idols in one form or another were used in many countries. The clever Chinese used quicksilver to effect their movements. Other idols and statues were made to move by natural mechanical means: counterbalance, clockwork, expansion of metal by heat, and the use of strings and wires. These idols were so well constructed and the operators were so accomplished that the movements, which were carefully hidden, were firmly believed to be of divine origin.

A description that has come down to us describes a miniature idol on an altar that was put in motion by steam power. A fire was lit on the altar, which contained a small tank of water. When the water got hot enough to turn into steam it was forced through a narrow tube which was connected with a vase in the idol's hand. The force of the steam was sufficient to tip the vase, bringing about a miraculous libation. Then amusements for the mass of people were precious few, and here and there enterprising men must have thought to themselves what a pity it was that so lively and theatrical a medium was confined to religious affairs.

Primitive puppet shows began to turn up in remote villages and at country fairs and markets. It seems logical to believe that the little man-like figures were patterned after the idols; their movements were similar but the showmen were clever enough to make their little actors less god-like. From the start they were enormously popular; at first they enacted familiar stories and legends, then as they acquired more polish and popularity they grew bolder and parodied current events and living people, usually their kings and queens, the detested tax-collector, or any notorious character.

In time they invaded the cities and quickly became the favorite amusement of all classes; in fact, the puppet became the voice of the people. They, safely enough, could air current abuses, make fun of the pretentious, celebrate valorous deeds, and spread the news.

But marionettes have never been content to stay in one place. Like all creative things they were restless and curious and constantly looking for new ideas and people to amuse. There are traces of wandering puppet showmen, with their portable booths, operating in Java, Burma, France, Spain, Germany, Russia, England, Turkey, Japan, Russia, Persia and India. Language was no barrier, the shows were broad enough in motion and familiar enough in story to be perfectly understandable when performed in pantomime.

In fact, there isn't a country in the world that didn't see the itinerant puppeteers. And, of course, as time went on and new materials were made available and new deeds were performed and new stories told, methods of production and presentation changed and were made to suit the characteristics of the land wherever the puppeteer found himself.

But then came the Dark Ages, which swallowed up in their

impenetrable fog the exploits of the marionette along with everything else. With the dawn of the Middle Ages the first glimpse of anything suggestive of the ancient art of puppetry appeared simultaneously with the earliest sculpture of the Ninth Century.

As the birth of the marionette was in the religious temples, its rebirth was in the church. The ecclesiasts in authority, in imitation of the high priests, were not content with just the sculptured figure of Christ, but employed ingenious artisans to construct figures on crosses that could be articulated. Contemporary writers have written of seeing statues that performed miraculous movements such as walking, gesticulating, and moving their eyes. Henri Maundrell, a pilgrim who visited the Holy Sepulchre in Jerusalem, tells of an assortment of mechanical figures, representing the various personages who took part in the life and crucifixion, that actually performed in every detail their parts, from the time when Christ is condemned up to the descent from the cross. Astonishing as it may seem, Maundrell claims such difficult details as the actual nailing to the cross were performed in full view of the pilgrims by these manikins who must have been just short of being human themselves.

History also mentions that the marionette makers who lived and worked in the Middle Ages were very wary about practicing their craft and exhibiting their marvels for the prudent reason that churchmen accused them of being in league with the devil. Many such unfortunate craftsmen and showmen were burned for practicing necromancy and witchcraft.

Gradually the authorities relaxed their restrictions, and with the opening of the Sixteenth Century marionettes became more and more a purely theatrical form of entertainment. Important events of the day were quickly adapted by shrewd impresarios as vehicles for their marionettes. There were no newspapers and radio to tell the people what was going on and marionettes proved an ideal medium. Where live actors couldn't dare make fun of the great, the puppets could and did without fear. For who could lower themselves to take a wooden figure seriously? Certainly not kings and tyrants. Or perhaps they didn't dare take away the popular entertainment from the people.

Only during the bloody French Revolution did most puppet booths lower their curtains. The few brave puppeteers who dared take part in the political controversies were imprisoned or forced to play slapstick or legendary stories.

Across the channel in England the beloved puppet Punch had been growing in popularity. Originally Punch was Polichinelle, the French puppet—and in all probability he, too, came over with William the Conqueror. He started with more bark than bite, but in time he assumed a purely British character and acquired such endearing habits in imitation of certain classes that the irreverent showmen portrayed him as Old Vice, Gluttony, Vanity, and Pride; and so the famous classic of Punch and Judy, mirroring the follies of the day, came into being.

In Europe marionettes endlessly portrayed the valorous deeds of the knights errant. The French romantic tales of the adventures of Charlemagne were ideally suited for the marionette theatre and were very popular. The deadly struggle between Saracen and Moor with the Christian knights made wonderfully exciting fare for the people of Southern Europe.

During all these centuries the Oriental countries, undisturbed by the bustling West, placidly developed the art of puppetry to its highest perfection. In rare wood, highly polished ivory and precious stone they made their figures and their greatest poets and playwrights fashioned their lines and action. The puppet box of the Orient holds many strange, exotic and lovely surprises for us. They entertain us not only with their pleasantries, but they also trouble our practical viewpoint with the mysticism of their creators. Even the marionettes seem to possess an impenetrable wisdom.

In the East there are many kinds of puppet shows, ranging from the most primitive to the most intricate. Many of the puppets are carved or fashioned with such skill that they may be compared to little gods in appearance and movement. Even the most primitive are executed with the great care and attention to detail characteristic of Oriental craftsmanship.

The chief difference between marionettes of the Orient and those of Europe is in temperament and point of view. Oriental puppets are gentle, shy, lovely, and rarely play practical jokes on their comrades. Western puppets tend to be grotesque, satirical, realistic and very practical.

But all puppets of the world are unmistakably bound together by a silken thread of kinship. They differ only in national characteristics. Italy, though, stands first in the number and variety of marionettes produced in Europe. They are found in every province and they vary in form and size and method of operation as do the local dialects themselves.

From the marionettes of Italy to those of France and Germany, Spain and England it is but a short step. The first marionettes in these countries were used to perform such religious themes as the Nativity and the Passion cycle. From there they progressed to more worldly shows playing the same plays as the legitimate theatres and mirroring the follies of the day. In France, particularly, they became a very popular form of entertainment with the people. Leading dramatists and poets wrote special plays for them and many became puppeteers themselves. George Sand and her son, Maurice, were ardent enthusiasts; they had a theatre at their chateau in Nohant and they wrote plays and put on performances regularly. A premiere performance attracted celebrities from all over France and they attended in the same spirit as they would a Parisian opening. George Sand created lovely costumes for the puppets, which still are preserved and can be seen in Paris. Among them is the famous figure of the melancholy Pierrot in his original white satin costume. Today the guignols (as the hand puppets are called) are still known in France, but the people who are showing them are no longer the artists of the earlier era and the performances are generally poor.

The situation in other European countries is a little better; the people didn't abandon their marionettes to the extent they have in sophisticated France. The old stylized marionette shows are given in exactly the same manner as they have been for centuries, and can be seen in most European countries. It is interesting to note that the brash American puppet has reversed the usual procedure and is threatening to replace the ancient European puppet—in Europe—in popularity.

When the great flood of emigration turned to America, the marionettes naturally came dancing along with the people. It is highly probable that marionettes already existed in the New World long before the white man arrived. Indian dolls, definitely articulated, have been preserved. They may have been used in religious ceremonies and tribal dances or some ingenious red-skinned father may have amused his little ones by making a doll that could be made to walk, bend and imitate human notions.

Punch and his comrades were among the first to arrive; but never once did he contemplate taking out citizenship papers—he always jealously kept his identity intact. He wasn't allowed on street corners here as he was in England, but his universal humor made an instant hit wherever he performed.

The emigrant German puppeteers, in their efforts to please new audiences, dropped their traditional plays and presented exhibitions of quick-moving stunts, tricks and transformation scenes—like changing a pumpkin into a horse and carriage in full view of the mystified audience—all very nice but a far cry from the lovely and exciting folk-tales and legends.

The Italian puppeteers, mostly Sicilians, were wiser. They set up shop among their own kind. They presented their stories, such as Orlando Furioso, which went on for century after century without a line or scene changed. Their audience expected nothing else—would have objected strenuously if it were different, and most important, there were no language bars to hurdle. The story lost nothing in the telling and for generations the Italian puppet theatre—a landmark in the alien land—looked exactly the same to the Italians in New York or Chicago as it did in Palermo. It might have been transplanted bodily out of the old country. It was intact even to benches, the flamboyant posters, the walls, the audience, the piano player and the stage itself.

All went along fine for a generation or so; then motion pictures grew more and more popular as a means of popular entertainment; and young and old, the literate and the uneducated, forsook the puppet shows and flocked to the new exciting movies.

But, of course, puppets, like all good troupers, never die. They bided their time and in bright spots all over the land they continued their antics and prayed for a better day. Today, mostly through the medium of television, plus the unswerving efforts of the faithful few, the marionette is again coming into his own, and again puppets and their making are a part of children's activities. Here in America, with more creative productions and experimentation, we may some day develop a national character worthy to take his place beside such woodenheads as Hanswurst, Casperl, Guignol, Peppenino, Larifari, Pulcinella, Karagheuz. and Punch.

BE A PUPPET SHOWMAN

⟨✧⟩

LET's begin by flatly assuming you know nothing—or next to nothing—about the making of puppets. It can be a surprising amount of fun and much simpler than you'd expect. The complicated secrets of the workshop eventually boil down to just using your common sense. What you need most is imagination, some mechanical ability, and a few basic tools: an inexpensive vise, a hand drill, a pocket and carving knives, a wood file, enthusiasm, a scroll saw, a wood chisel, a hammer, and soft wood will see you through just about everything we are going to ask you to do.

Building a puppet

Our logical starting point is the puppet itself. Plan on making him fifteen inches from the top of his head to the bottom of his torso. You'll find this size easily manageable and, besides, it will give the illusion of being life-size to your audience. But before you begin any cutting it would be wise to make a rough drawing of the entire puppet to guide you. After you have done this, stand back and calculate the size of the figure's head, which is the first thing to make. For the size puppet you're about to make, the head should be about five inches from top to bottom, or approximately one-third of the torso without the legs, which we shall explain about later.

Making the head

Use a block of wood five inches long, three inches wide, and three inches thick. Bore a hole in one end about an inch and

Block with head outlined
and hole bored in neck

Block in vise

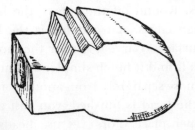

Profile of head cut
from block

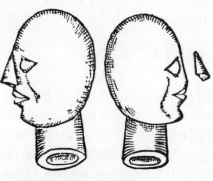

Complete head with
and without nose

CARVING A WOODEN HEAD

a half deep and wide enough to allow the second, or index, finger to fit in freely. This will be the bottom of your puppet's neck. Then draw a profile of the head on the thick side of the block, as well as an outline of the face on the front of the block. Now set the block of wood in your vise and cut below the chin with your carving knife to the neckline and then chip away the excess wood below the chin—being very careful with your knife. Repeat the same operation at the back of the head and also at the two sides. Keep cutting away with your chisel, pocket, or carving knife—but be sure not to cut too much—let your pattern be your guide, and you'll find in a very short time that your block is miraculously taking on the form of a head.

Your next step will be to scoop out hollows above the cheeks for making the eyes. Round off the top of the head by whittling away the rough edges. A wood file is the best tool for making rounded surfaces. Carve a slit for the mouth and round off the chin. You'll find it much simpler and much more practical to make the nose separately from another small piece of wood; and when the head is finished, you just glue the nose on it in the proper place. For eyes use beads or buttons. Now all you have to do is to smooth off the entire head with a square of fine sandpaper and go on to making the hands.

Making the hands

Use a block eight inches long, two inches wide, and one inch thick. You probably will have to cut your wood to the sizes specified, but this is a very simple matter. Mark on the wide surface each hand (right and left). It is much more practical to carve both hands from the one block of wood—this prevents the common mistake of carving two right or two left hands, a mistake that even experts make. Place the block

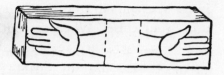

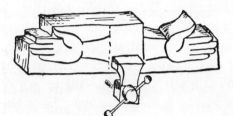

Hands on block

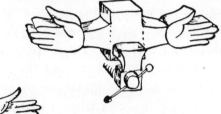

Final stages

MAKING THE HANDS

in the vise and cut to the markings as shown in the drawing, using your chisel. When the outlines of both hands are cut in this manner, turn the block upside-down in the vise so that you can shape the thickness of the hands. When one hand is done, reverse the block in the vise and work on the other exactly in the same manner. Try to make both hands as nearly alike as possible. Stop carving when you have reached the final thickness and general shape of the hand. Now mark out the fingers with a pencil, draw the edge of your knife along the lines, and dig out a "V" the full length of each finger. Repeat this on both sides and you have the rounded fingers, as the drawing shows. When this is done you can saw apart the two hands and shave down the wrists to the thickness of your own middle finger. Sandpaper as you did the head. You're not quite finished—the hands must have tubes attached to the wrists, these tubes are eventually used for the manipulation of the puppet's hands. They are simply made by cutting two pieces of ordinary wrapping paper two inches by six inches and smearing them on both sides with a good sticking paste: a mixture of library paste and Le Page's glue is excellent. Smear the wrist with paste, wrap the paper around it, and bind tightly with ordinary sewing thread.

Making the body

Now you've finished with the head and arms. The body is the next step. This is simply a sleeve made of any light and strong material and designed to fit over your hand and fore-arm, with three openings (see drawing on assembling the puppet). Mark out your pattern on a piece of paper (see drawing). Make certain the pattern is symmetrical by folding it in half. Make the approximate size of the body pattern, without the arms and neck, fifteen inches long, six inches wide

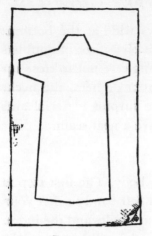

Pattern

Hand in puppet body

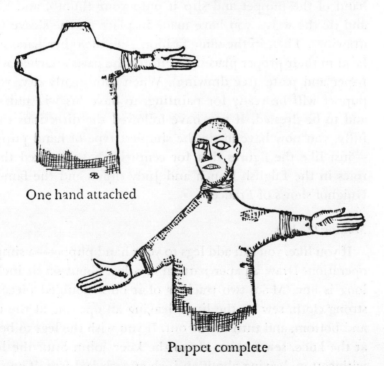

One hand attached

Puppet complete

ASSEMBLING THE PUPPET

15

across the shoulders, and seven inches wide at the bottom. Now that you have the pattern, place it on a piece of doubled material, trace it, sew on the line, taking care not to close up the four necessary openings, the bottom or hem, the neck, and the two arms. Now cut away the surplus material and turn the body inside out, so it will have a neat seam.

Assembling the body

Now you have the head, arms, and body. The first step is to draw the sleeve-like body over your left hand so that your thumb and middle finger slip into the armholes and the index finger into the neck hole, as in drawing. Take the right hand of the puppet and slip it onto your thumb, and glue and tie the wrists you have made in place on the sleeve (see drawing). Then in the same fashion glue the other hand and head in their proper places. Reinforce the parts attached with paper and paste (see drawing). When thoroughly dry, your puppet will be ready for painting, to have his wig put on, and to be dressed. If you have followed the directions carefully, you now have made the simplest type of hand puppet —just like the figures that for centuries have enacted their roles in the English Punch and Judy shows and the famous Guignol shows of France.

Making the legs

If you like, you can add legs to your hand puppet—a simple operation. Draw a paper pattern of a leg, about seven inches long is fine. Make two tracings of it on a doubled piece of strong cloth, sew on the lines, leaving an opening at the top and bottom, and turn inside out. If you wish the legs to bend at the knee, sew a seam across the knee joint. Stuff the legs with cotton, leaving about an inch at each end free. The feet can be carved of wood and glued to the cloth ankles; simpler

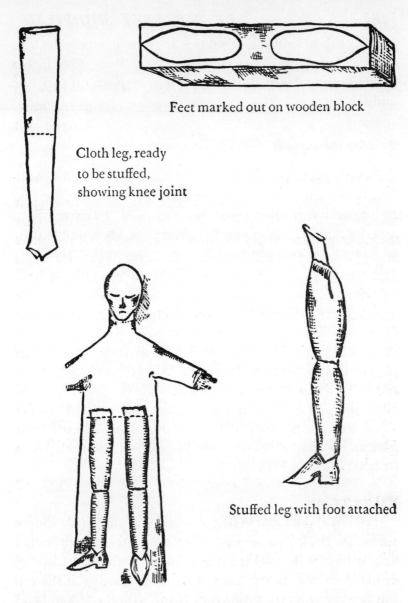

Feet marked out on wooden block

Cloth leg, ready
to be stuffed,
showing knee joint

Stuffed leg with foot attached

Puppet with legs sewed in place

MAKING THE LEGS

still is a pair of stuffed doll's shoes. In order to attach the legs, draw a line across the front of the body about four inches below the shoulders. Pin the two legs in place on this line and sew them securely.

Painting the puppet

Now that your puppet is assembled, you are ready for painting. Show-card colors should be used for this. They are easy to handle, inexpensive, come in a variety of attractive colors, and dry rapidly. While painting, there are a few simple rules to follow: Always keep your brushes clean so that you don't mix one color with another, and apply paint only on a *dry* surface.

To obtain a flesh color, mix some white with a touch of red and yellow. When colors get thick in the jar, add enough water to thin them. Before painting the face, mark out in pencil the shape of the mouth and eyes, and hair line. Apply the flesh color you have just mixed, leaving unpainted those spaces you have marked out in pencil. When the face is dry, paint the eyeballs white and the lips red. Then paint the eyelashes and the eyebrows in any color you prefer. A very fine black line around the lips will make them more distinct. You might paint in the pupils of the eyes rather than use beads.

The color you have used on the face will do for the hands with dabs of white outlined in black for the fingernails. Paint the feet whatever color you think goes best with the puppet's costume. As for the hair, you can simply paint it on, but more theatrical and effective are bits of fur or strands of bright-colored knitting wool or embroidery silk glued in rows on the head. Unraveled hempen rope makes splendid wigs.

Fur   Wool   Rope

WIGS

Costumes

Don't be afraid to use your imagination and sense of color in designing the puppet's costume; the stage will be immeasurably brightened and gayer by colorful costumes. Solid colors are best. If figured materials are used, make sure the design is small. But, since the puppet must be worn on the hand, you can see, naturally, how the design of the costume must remain within prescribed limits. For instance, do not make a waistline that will be too small to fit around the operator's wrist. Remember the unavoidable sleeve which is part of the puppet. The costume should help make that as inconspicuous as possible. Lady puppets with long skirts hide the sleeve successfully. Wide trousers, long-tail coats, voluminous smocks, tunics, and cloaks help conceal the puppet's sleeve. Remember, too, that if the lower part of the puppet's sleeve is covered with the same material as the garment next to it, it will give the impression of being all part of the outfit.

Make a rough sketch of your puppet in costume. Decide on how many pieces there are to be and make the patterns.

Let the basic pattern of the puppet's body be your guide for the costume pattern. This will insure the costume's fitting well. An ill-fitting costume will ruin a good puppet and make it move badly. Take as much time and thought in making your costume as you did with your puppet. The materials you use should be chosen with an eye for the hanging and non-fraying qualities. Costumes that are lined always hang better. If you have any trouble, insert small weights in the hem of your costume. Cloaks and trains, by the way, can be made to swing very effectively by the use of weights.

For example, let us start with Cinderella, a lady puppet. We wish to dress her for the ball at the prince's palace. Before cutting your material, make an accurate paper pattern. If you will examine the illustrated pattern for Cinderella's costume, you will see that every pattern strictly adheres to the master sleeve, or body, pattern. Note that the armholes, neckline, and the waist are wide enough so that the costume fits loosely over the puppet body, allowing it freedom of motion. The jacket and the girdle should be lined. You might find it helpful to give Cinderella a petticoat. When all the pieces of the costume are made, sew them in place firmly to the foundation sleeve, or body, of the puppet. Then open your treasure box and see what jewels and precious stones you can find to add to Cinderella's beauty. Now she is ready to step into her pumpkin coach and be whisked off to the prince's ball.

The next step is to dress the prince. Design a costume to fit his rank—something dashing and regal. Choose your material carefully and use a paper pattern to guide you. A pleasant combination might be to make his coat and breeches of a green silk, his cloak of black velvet (sew lead weights between the lining and the velvet) lined with yellow silk, his boots and hat of black shiny oilcloth. Now that you are fairly adept at making costumes, you may use your judgment in designing

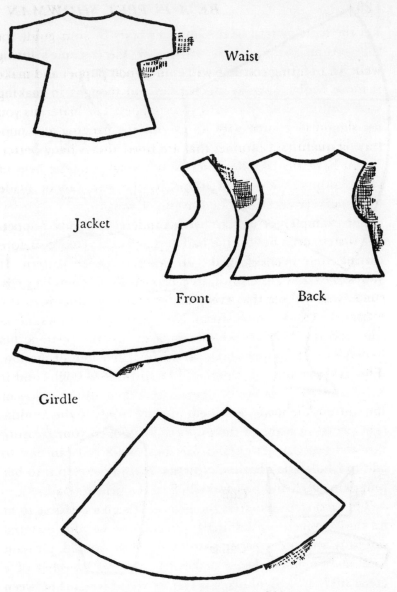

Waist

Jacket

Front   Back

Girdle

Skirt (*four sections like this*)

PATTERNS FOR CINDERELLA'S COSTUME

21

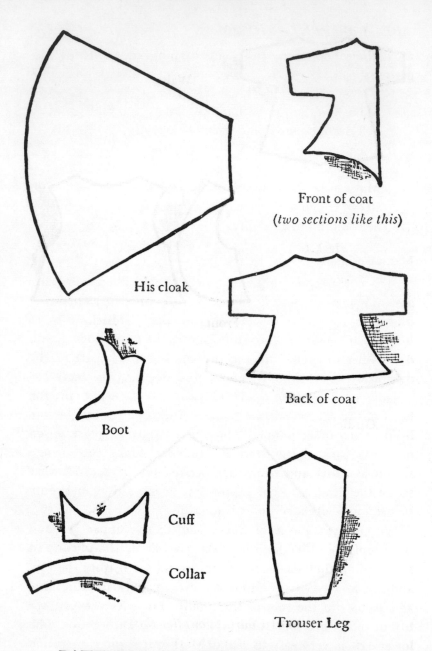

Front of coat
(*two sections like this*)

His cloak

Back of coat

Boot

Cuff

Collar

Trouser Leg

PATTERNS FOR PRINCE'S COSTUME

22

any others you need. Just keep in mind these useful suggestions:

1. Make your costume simple in design.
2. Select your color combinations carefully.
3. Use practical materials.
4. Cut patterns carefully.
5. Make sure the costume fits freely over the foundation sleeve which is the body of the puppet.
6. Sew and finish carefully.

Making animals

Why not try your hand on puppet animals? They are always amusing and very effective—and not too difficult to make. A dragon is exciting. You can make one that writhes and snaps his jaws ferociously. You follow along the same lines as you did with Cinderella and the prince. The main part of the dragon's body will be the foundation sleeve. This sleeve has a wider neck opening than those you have already cut; the head of the dragon will be fitted in the same opening as the head of any other puppet. The tail is a separate piece sewed onto the back of the foundation sleeve. Make your rough sketch as usual and from that decide how large and what shape the head is to be. Suppose we make a dragon twenty inches long with a seven-inch long head.

We take two pieces of wood, one for the upper jaw and head and the other for the lower jaw. Draw the outline of the head on the first block, as you would see it from the top, and cut away. Carve hollows for eyes, a ridge for the nose, and scoop out the roof of the mouth. For eyes you can use bright red or green glass buttons; for teeth, white beads. The lower jaw is very easy to make. Mark out a piece to match the upper jaw and scoop out the inside.

The next step is to hinge the two jaws together so that they will open and close. This is done by nailing two strips of leather to both sides of the jaws inside the mouth. When the carving and hinging are finished, attach the head to the sleeve with glue and tacks so that it comes inside the upper jaw and outside the lower one. This will keep the top of the head clean-cut and blend the lower jaw into the neck. Make the claws out of unbleached muslin, stuff with cotton, and finish with the heavy paper, paste, and thread, as has been described for the hands. Then sew them to the two armholes below the neck. If you feel that the dragon needs more than two legs—and what self-respecting dragon doesn't—you can make and attach any number anywhere down the length of the body. Make the tail of unbleached muslin, stuff it, and sew it to the back of the body about nine or ten inches from the head. You can make it wriggle and lash impressively by attaching a stiff wire an inch or two from the tail end.

There are no costume problems with an animal puppet; painting it brilliantly is all that is necessary—use bright greens, reds, and yellows. To paint cloth without stiffening it, use either colored inks or dyes. If you wish to paint scales, outline them with melted wax. Then take your inks or dyes and paint inside the waxed outlines. Since the head is of wood, paint it with the same show-card colors you used for Cinderella.

The animal world is wide: cats, dogs, frogs, alligators, elephants, fish, and birds. You can make any of these as easily as you made the dragon. Every animal, you know, has its own individual peculiarities; and if you catch these idiosyncrasies, the smaller details, you will find, will take care of themselves.

Another interesting type of animal puppet is the kind that is held on the stage at the end of a stick. An elephant is a

Wooden head

Stuffed tail

Stuffed claws

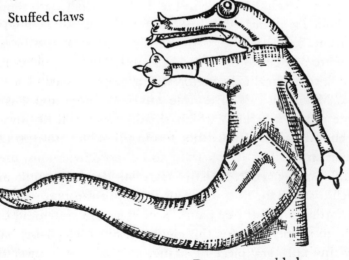

Dragon assembled

MAKING A DRAGON

25

good example. The chief advantage of this type is that you have no sleeve problem and it shows the complete form of the animal. The stick you disguise with paint, attaching it so that the elephant's legs conceal it.

As usual, make your working sketch. To make an elephant twelve inches long—not including the trunk or the tail—use a piece of wood about seven inches long by one inch square. This will be the foundation of the body. Drill a vertical hole in it a quarter-inch in diameter about two inches from one end. Into this fit a quarter-inch dowel stick, fifteen inches long. This will serve to hold the figure. Glue and nail it into place. Dowel sticks of all sizes can be bought at any hardware store. This completes the foundation of the body and the means of manipulation.

A fine material for an elephant is a gray cotton duvetyn which will look like real elephant skin from the front. Cut a body pattern like the one in the drawing; the length should be about eight inches. When your material is cut, sew up the front, back, and top, turn it inside out, stuff it, and tack the bottom edges to the wooden foundation. A wooden ball about two inches in diameter will answer perfectly for the head. Make the ears of double duvetyn, sewed and turned inside out. The trunk, which should taper a little toward the end, should be stuffed not too firmly with cotton so that it remains flexible. If you want to be more ingenious, use a flexible spring, covered with material, for the trunk and attach a stiff wire to the end of it so you can wave it back and forth with your free hand. Now search in your bead box again to supply eyes for the elephant. Since elephants have very tiny tails, any piece of string, painted, will answer the purpose.

While you are painting the tail you might also paint the head. Now take a strip of cloth about two inches wide and

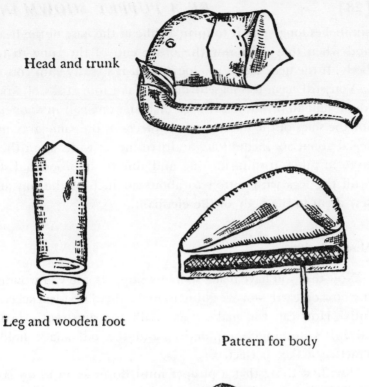

Head and trunk

Leg and wooden foot

Pattern for body

Elephant assembled

MAKING AN ELEPHANT

six inches long, glue it to form a tube at the base of the head, and when that dries sew the other end of the tube to the body. If the neck seems too loose, stuff it slightly with cotton.

You still have the legs to make. Take four disks of wood about half an inch thick and an inch and one-half in diameter for the soles of the feet. Cut four pieces of the same gray material about six inches long and five inches wide, seam them to form tubes, turn inside out, and glue to the wooden disks. Stuff the legs with cotton to about an inch of the top and sew them to the body of the elephant.

Manipulation

Now that you have made so many puppets, are you wondering how on earth you are going to make them perform successfully? How can you make them walk and apparently really talk? It's nothing but practice, and the old adage holds: Practice makes perfect.

The first thing that a puppet must do or seem to do is—walk. This is how it is done. Put the puppet on either hand so that you can control the head and arms comfortably with the three first fingers. Raise it until the feet stand on a shelf above your head. By turning the wrist from left to right as you advance it in rhythmical jerks and also raising and lowering it slightly, the puppet will give a definite impression of walking. To make a step involves three distinct movements all at one time (don't be alarmed) turning the wrist from left to right, advancing it in even jerks, raising, and lowering it. The turning of the wrist has a tendency to swing the leg, the jerking throws it forward, the raising of the wrist takes it off the floor, and the lowering of the wrist takes it back to the floor in an advanced position. Try it. Practice it constantly. You'll be surprised how quickly you can master this

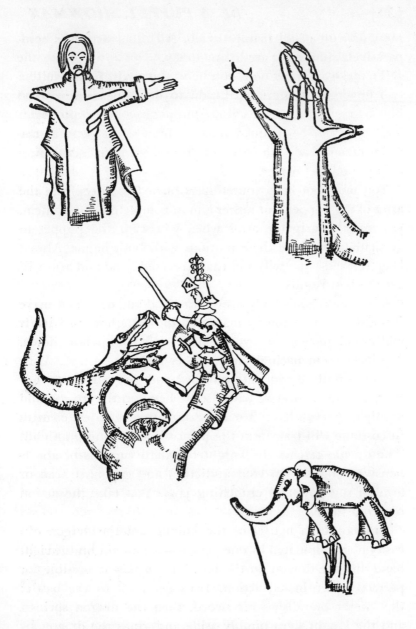

MANIPULATION OF PUPPETS

most difficult of all manipulation. All other action is com-
paratively simple, we are happy to say.

To make a puppet bow, you bend your wrist forward. The
two fingers in the arms can add to the appearance of the
bow by moving the hands of the puppet in graceful positions.
The head can be inclined forward by a slight bend of the
index-finger inside the neck. Try it and see what a charming
bow the puppet makes.

You must not keep your fingers buried too deeply in the
arms of the puppet, but rather almost completely out of them,
yet ready to grip the arms when you want the puppet to
gesticulate. Practice these motions with both hands. Always
keep relaxed—you will find that a relaxed hand and arm will
get the best results.

Slip the dragon's body over your hand and arm, and make
it wriggle and writhe by manipulating your fingers. Give it
additional movement by working its jaws up and down,
flap its claws menacingly at the other puppets onstage. Your
audience will be completely baffled and delighted. You can
stage a simple, effective battle scene between the dragon and
a knight. (If you haven't made extra puppets, a few changes
in costume will transform the prince into a shining knight.)
The dragon catches the knight off-guard (squeals of appre-
hensive delight from your audience) and grips his head or
arm in the powerful crunching jaws. You take the action
on from there.

Anyway, both figures of the knight and the dragon can
easily be manipulated by one person—the knight on the right
hand and the dragon on the left. This makes it possible for
perfectly coordinated action. Let's get back to the battle:
the knight brandishes his sword, then the dragon springs,
and the knight steps nimbly aside and grabs the dragon by
the tail, the dragon turns swiftly and grapples with the knight

—you can make them roll all over the stage in each other's arms.

The knight is visibly weakening—the dragon snaps his jaws closer and closer to the knight's head. But with a supreme effort the knight throws off the dragon and thrusts his sword into the dragon's obligingly open mouth. The dragon gives several violent contortions and slowly and thumpingly expires.

This is how you work this scene: grip the index-finger of your right hand with the fingers of your left hand, thus controlling the dragon's mouth. The whole battle, simply, is one between your right hand and your left. After this practice, you'll be surprised how life-like the puppets behave and how easy it is to acquire the skill to make them do what you want them to do. You won't need detailed instructions about the working of puppet animals on sticks. You have probably found out how simple it really is. The important thing to watch is that the stick is held perpendicular and high enough so the feet of the puppet move across and on the stage floor. Try it a few times and see for yourself how it works.

But to do all these exciting things you must have a stage for your puppets to perform their valorous deeds. Take your choice: you can either build a simple theatre with a minimum of materials or, if that isn't practical and if you're pressed for time, you can give your performance on top of a fairly large table. Drape a dark cloth over the table which will reach to the floor and hide you from the audience. You, of course, will have to either kneel or sit on the floor behind the table. You'll be surprised how much of the illusion is still retained by this simple form of staging. But if you are willing to spend a little time and energy you can easily build a practical and attractive working theatre.

Making the theatre

The first thing your stage must have is a proscenium, which is nothing more than a frame-like opening for your performing puppets. In other words, the audience sees your show through a picture frame. A puppet theatre must also have a shelf, which makes a floor for the puppets to walk on. The third essential is a background or scene, and, last of all, some sort of lighting—as simple or as complicated as you wish.

There are three basic positions from which the manipulators can choose in working the action. You can either stand up, sit down, or kneel. Try them all and find which is the most comfortable for you and plan the height of your theatre so that the bottom of the proscenium comes at the top of your head, whatever your position may be.

Supposing you prefer to work in a standing position and you want to make your theatre quickly and with the minimum of material. The simplest plan for a puppet theatre is a screen that has three panels. Measure off and cut your proscenium in the middle panel. If your puppets are two feet high, make your proscenium opening not less than two and one-half feet high. Get two light metal brackets at a hardware store, screw them to the wooden framework of your center panel inside the proscenium and just below it. Then fasten a board across the brackets to form the stage floor. Make this shelf six inches wide and a few inches longer than the length of the proscenium. It must also be level with the bottom of the proscenium so that the feet of the puppets may be seen by the audience. Stand your screen upright. Fold the two side panels back until they are at right angles to the middle panel. Nail a stick across the back at the top of the two side panels. This will steady the whole structure

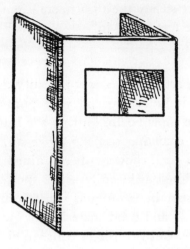

Screen with proscenium cut out

Rear view of stage

MAKING A SIMPLE THEATRE

and also provide a place from which to hang your background. If this stick does not steady the theatre sufficiently, nail another stick about three feet below it.

The curtain

Now for your curtain—apart from its mute beauty and promise of magic to come—it hides you and your puppets from the audience before the show begins, during the intermission, and while you are changing scenes. Above all, it must work smoothly. Many a good show has been ruined by a curtain that opened and closed awkwardly—thus spoiling the illusion. Rehearse your curtain as often as you rehearse your puppets. Select some soft and solid material for it. A bright color is always effective. Cut two pieces equal to eight inches, or more than half the width of the proscenium and two inches longer than its height, and allowing enough for hems on all four sides. Sew about half a dozen little brass rings along the top of each curtain.

Now comes the rigging of the curtain, which means hanging it in place and fixing it so that you can easily pull it open and shut. Rig your curtain on the panel above the proscenium or on a separate strip of wood. The top of the curtain should be about two inches above the top of the proscenium, so that the audience does not see the rings. The rings will slide more easily on a taut wire. Hang the bottom of the curtain half an inch above the shelf floor, so that it will not drag.

Slip a wire through all the rings and fasten it taut across the top of the proscenium by means of screw-eyes at each end. Slide your curtains back and forth to make sure there is no serious sag in the wire. At the left side, about an inch beyond the screw-eye which holds the curtain wire, put a second larger screw, and an inch beyond that a third large screw-eye. On the right side, as the drawing shows, about an inch be-

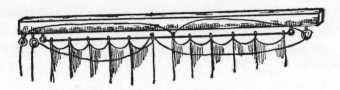

Detail of curtain rigging

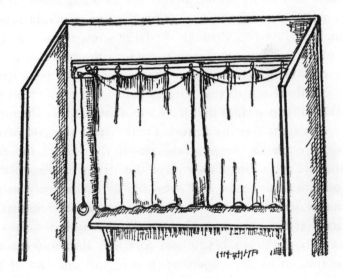

Curtain in place

A DRAW CURTAIN

yond the screw-eye which holds the curtain wire, place a larger screw-eye. Now compare your work with the illustration showing the detail of the curtain rigging to make certain that your screw-eyes are properly placed. If you are satisfied all is properly placed, go ahead and rig your curtain. First close and center the curtain. Then take a piece of strong twine about two and a half times the length and height of your proscenium. Wax the twine and tie one end, temporarily, to a nail at the bottom of the left side of the proscenium. Next take the loose end of the twine and thread it through the middle screw-eye on the left side of the proscenium. Pull the string taut and tie it to the last ring of the left curtain, which is now at the center. Make sure in doing this that you do not pull the curtain away from the center of the proscenium. Pass the string through the large screw-eye at the right side of the proscenium, bring it back to the last ring of the right curtain, which is also at the center. Make your string taut and tie it fast to this ring as you did the other on the left side. The two rings that have the string tied to them now meet very tightly at the center. Finally, pass the end of the string through the large screw-eyes at the left of the proscenium. Try pulling this end of the string to see whether the middle rings center and press tightly against each other. Now that your curtain is rigged, untie the end fastened to the nail (at the bottom of the left side). Attach a weight to each end of the string. If you have followed directions exactly, the curtains will draw open when you pull one end of the string and close when you pull the other.

Lighting

You now have your theatre—complete with working curtains—and an assortment of puppets. Now you must have some kind of light for your stage so the puppets can be seen.

For all practical purposes an ordinary desk lamp will do. The best place to spot it is at the top of your theatre. Nail a board across the roof, fasten your lamp on it, and direct the light where it will do the most good. Get someone to stand out front and tell you at what point the lamp gives the most effective light.

Background

Now the only thing lacking in your theatre is the background. A simple suggestion—for a permanent background—take a piece of light blue or gray cloth long enough to go around the sides and back of the stage space and wide enough to reach the roof of the theatre to a point level with the bottom of the proscenium. Effective pieces of scenery can be cut out of cardboard, painted with show-card colors, and hung from the strip of wood across the back of the proscenium in front of your permanent background.

A more professional theatre

Some of you who are more skilled with tools may be interested in building a larger and more permanent type of theatre—one that would satisfy professional standards. There are no arbitrary measurements for a puppet theatre. Its size depends on what space you have available, the size of your puppets, and the size of your expected audience. Suppose your puppets average two feet in height, an adequate size for your theatre would be seven feet high, seven feet wide, and three and a half feet deep. Use correspondingly proportionate measurements for various sizes of theatres.

For practical purposes we are going to build a seven-foot theatre. The first step is to plan it out carefully on paper— avoid guesswork and save time and material. When you have all your measurements, order your lumber. Specify strips of pine two inches wide by three-fourths of an inch thick, and see that it is straight and smooth and easy to work with. The complete framework of the theatre is made up of four separate screens—one for the front, one for each side, and one for the back.

Make your screens first. For the front screen cut six lengths of lumber seven feet long and two lengths five feet long. Nail them together, as shown in the illustration, so that your proscenium opening is five feet long and three feet high. Plan to manipulate your puppets from a sitting position, in which case the bottom of your proscenium should be approximately forty-six inches from the floor. For each side screen cut two lengths of wood seven feet long and three lengths three and a half feet long, and nail together, again following the illustration. For the back screen use two seven-foot lengths and three four-foot lengths. Nail the short pieces between the long ones exactly as you did in your side screens. Now your four screens are complete and the framework is ready to be assembled. Use nails if you want your framework to be permanent, but if you prefer it to be demountable and portable, use screws and loose pin hinges. Fasten the two side screens to the front—one to the right and one to the left side. The screen for the back fits flush with the top of the side screens. If the completed framework is unsteady, you can put diagonal braces in the individual screens wherever needed. So much for the outside structure. Before covering the framework, you must complete the inside of your equipment.

The stage comes first. For this use a plank six feet long and about four inches wide and three-fourths of an inch thick. You will find it very useful to equip at least one side of it with a set of slots, so that you will be able to fix pieces of scenery and stage properties in it. To make these slots take

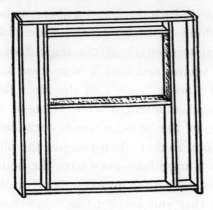

Front frame

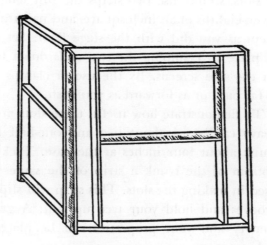

Front and side frame

FRAMEWORK OF A THEATRE

several pieces of wood about three inches long, three-fourths of an inch wide and a quarter-inch thick and nail them about three inches apart all along one edge of the wide plank. Take another strip equal the length of the stage floor by three-fourths of an inch square and nail it over these short strips so that a series of slots is formed in the stage floor. Then take two metal brackets about a foot in length and fasten these with screws to the wooden framework below each side of the proscenium, so that when you put the plank across them, it will make a stage floor even with the bottom of the proscenium. When you secure the stage floor in place to the brackets, be sure that you leave a space between it and the proscenium for the curtains to ride in. A row of slots can also be used across the extreme back of your stage for trees, houses, and other stage accessories. In making this set of slots, simply use two strips the full length of your stage, seven-eighths of an inch square, and nail thin pieces between them as you did with the stage floor. Set this row of slots in place by clamping the two ends down to the cross piece on the side screens. By the use of clamps you can place it as far back or as forward as you wish.

To demonstrate how useful these slots are, make a tree of heavy cardboard about two and one-half feet high with a trunk about four inches at the base. Tack and glue to the bottom of the trunk a strip of the same wood which you used in making the slots. This strip will slip into any of your grooves and hold your tree upright. A great deal of your scenery and your properties can be placed in this handy fashion.

For a background or backdrop you can use much the same kind of cloth as you did in the smaller theatre. There are other backdrops, too, the kinds that are painted like real theatrical scenery; you'll find a full description of this type of scenery in the following chapter.

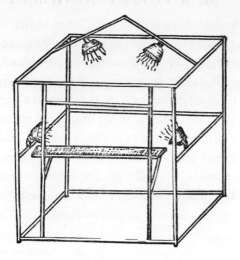

Front view

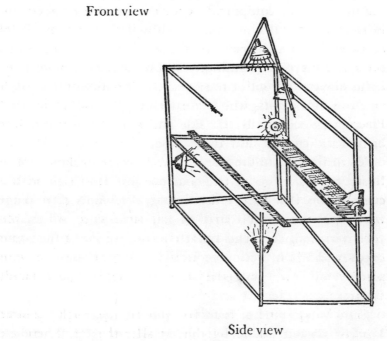

Side view

ASSEMBLED FRAMEWORK

You already know that a curtain parts in the middle. If you decide to use that type in this more elaborate equipment, rig it on a separate strip of wood and hook the whole rigging in place so that you can dismantle it if you need to. Not only your curtain, but the entire framework of this theatre can be easily dismantled and stacked in a corner out of the way if you make use of pin hinges and screws, instead of nails, in putting the screen units together. Then there is the kind of curtain which rolls up and down. If you are interested in making this, you will find complete directions in the next chapter.

Lighting

Any electrical equipment requiring the use of a switchboard, and units that are controlled by it, should be made by an experienced electrician. If you decide you must have this professional type of lighting, plan on having a row of footlights along the front of the proscenium outside the curtain and two side lights, which are technically called "floods." Place one flood at the left side and one at the right, just behind the curtain near the bottom of the proscenium, in order to illuminate the stage fully. If you can afford more than that, try a few more floods overhead just behind the curtain line. All these units should have individual plugs which are controlled from a switchboard. This will enable you to have all the lights on at once, or as few as the scene requires. The illustration shows clearly how these lights are placed and how neatly the whole system can be devised. If this rather extensive and expensive equipment is impractical for you to set up, you can figure out something almost as effective and usable by the use of several simple desk lamps.

The only thing left before you start your show is to close

in the framework of your theatre neatly, so that all your backstage is hidden from the curious eyes of your audience. It is always wise to warn your audience before you pull the curtain up by following the time-honored custom of striking a bell three times. The Guignol shows on the Champs Elysees in Paris begin in this fashion: A hand is thrust outside the booth with a large bell which is rung until all the children have gathered eagerly to see the show. Then the bell stops. There is a great watchful silence. Then this silence is broken by another bell, which tinkles away as the curtain slowly rises. But it looks and sounds as if your curtain were rising, so let's sit back and watch.

MARIONETTES

-<✦>-

STRINGS ARE JUST AS EASY

WE assume by this time that you've discovered the thrill and satisfaction that comes from giving a successful show. Your puppets have responded beautifully, your theatre is still in one piece—and your audience has had the most wonderful and exciting time.

So—if you're looking for new worlds to conquer, consider the marionette. Marionettes differ from hand puppets in that they are worked by strings from above. Also, marionettes are made differently, as is the marionette theatre. Certainly the making of a marionette show is more difficult—but it is far from insurmountable. One attraction is that marionettes are less strenuous to work than puppets as you work them from above, which is much easier on your back and knees. So if you'd like to try making a marionette show, come along with us.

There are four different types of marionettes which you can make; one kind is rather easy to make, the others a little more complicated. First, there is the simple stuffed figure, which is made entirely of cloth and stuffed, then there is the marionette made of wood, the figure made of papier-maché, and the marionette made of plastic wood. The general principle, however, remains the same in all four types.

In any case, a good marionette must be very loosely jointed. The arms, legs, head, and body will then respond easily to the pulling of strings. This principle distinguishes marionettes from ordinary dolls.

Suppose we forget temporarily about the more difficult types and start with the simple stuffed figure.

Making a stuffed marionette

All you need is unbleached muslin and stuffing, a little skill in sewing, and a pair of scissors. Make a guide drawing of the figure first, then cut separate paper patterns for the head, body, arms, legs, and feet. Trace the pieces on your muslin, and cut to the desired shapes, sew them, and turn them inside out. Stuff the pieces with cotton, leaving both narrow extensions unstuffed. Sew these extensions together, keeping the torso flexible. Stuff the head, leaving unstuffed half an inch of the neck, and then sew it to the body.

The arms will move better if they are filled with something heavier than cotton. Metal beads are best for this purpose. Stuff these beads into the hand, then wind thread tightly around the wrist and drop in more beads to reach the elbow. Wind your string tightly around the elbow, too. Then fill the rest of the arm with more beads to within an inch of the shoulder. Sew the arms to the shoulders.

Fill the feet with cotton and beads, too, and sew them crosswise to the bottom of the legs, thereby making flexible ankles. In order to have the marionette stand firmly and walk well, the lower part of the legs should be well weighted. Therefore, also fill the leg to the knee with your mixture of cotton and beads. Sew across the knee as you did across the ankle, then stuff the remaining part of the leg with cotton, again leaving the last inch unstuffed. Now join the legs in place to the body. When assembled, the arms and legs of your marionette should swing like pendulums when dangled in the air. If they do, you will then know that all parts have been properly weighted and loosely jointed. If they don't, check your work carefully—probably only a minor error that you can correct easily.

Using show-card colors, you can begin to paint those parts of the marionette which will show after it is dressed: the arms and legs. For the head you must use colored inks. The arms and legs are painted in flesh colors. However, be careful to leave the joints in every case unpainted, so as not to stiffen them. Draw black lines to indicate fingers and color the fingernails with white. In making the wig, wool yarn or embroidery silk or unraveled rope will serve you as well. Any of these you can easily sew to the head.

Your marionette made of cloth and ready to be strung is still without a costume. You must know Pierrot, the most famous marionette for centuries past. Why not make this one a Pierrot with a romantic white face and a black skull cap which comes to a point on his forehead. His costume is simple as well as picturesque.

His clothing is all white. Soft silk, or white sateen will do very nicely. Cut a pattern for the coat, with sleeves attached. Trace this on a doubled cloth, cut, sew, and turn it. The coat should open up the front and have a row of black pompons sewed from the neck to the bottom. Also attach one pompon to each sleeve. You can make realistic pompons out of black yarn by tying several strands together and cutting them off short so that they look like tiny whisk brooms. Sew up the trousers from a pattern, turn them, and attach pompons at the very bottom.

Pierrot usually has a ruff. To make this, take a long one-inch-wide strip of the same material you have been using and gather it onto the band which fits around the figure's neck, and there you are. Take an old black silk stocking, fit it tight to Pierrot's head, seam it, and gather it in at the top, and you have his skull cap. Make sure that the costume fits loosely enough so that all his joints can move as easily as before he had any clothes on.

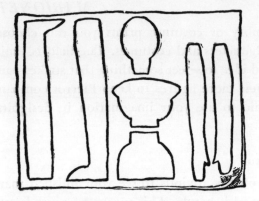

Patterns for parts

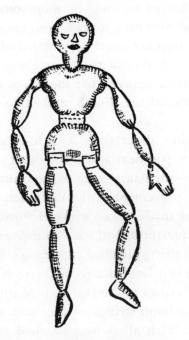

An arm and
leg finished

Assembled figure

A STUFFED MARIONETTE

47

From memory or costume prints you can choose other marionette characters and costumes. The field is limitless. It may be a good idea to select something that strikes your fancy and make a few more figures to keep Pierrot company. And don't be afraid to use your imagination in designing their costumes.

A simple control

You are probably anxious to see your finished marionette walk and move his hands. This means he must be strung— don't be alarmed, this is not as dire as it sounds. The number of strings necessary for the manipulation varies; it depends on how many different motions you want your figure to make. Seven strings is all you need to make your marionette come to obedient life. Strings are attached to the vital places on your figure: one on each side of the head about where the ears are, one on the back between the shoulders, one on the back of each hand toward the thumb, and one on each knee.

Sew a nylon fishing line about three feet long at each of these places. This done, you next attach the other ends of the strings to a "control"—the name given to the contrivance which really *controls* the movement of the marionette.

A simple control can be made of two sticks of wood about eight inches long and a quarter-inch thick. To the center of one of these sticks tie the string attached to the back of your marionette. Then tie the two head strings to the ends of the same stick. Tie the knee strings to the two ends of the other stick and then tie the two hand strings on the same stick at an equal distance apart. With all strings attached and the figure relaxed, both sticks should meet at the same height. At the same time all the strings must be taut.

A ring, tied near the top of the back strings, helps lift the

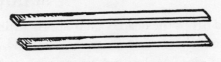

The control—two sticks

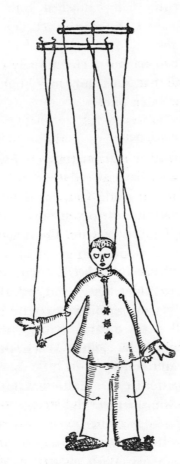

Pierrot on strings

A SIMPLE CONTROL

shoulders and drops the head. Catch the ring with your thumb while holding the stick in the same hand. Move the head from side to side by tipping the stick up and down. You make the marionette walk by tipping the other stick up and down and advancing it forward slightly each time. You raise the hands by simply pulling the strings attached to them.

Stringed marionettes can easily get tangled. When not using them, keep them safe and out of harm's way by hooking both sticks over two nails driven into any convenient wall. When you've done that, start thinking about the second type of marionette, a wooden one.

Making a wooden marionette

In making a wooden marionette, you follow an entirely different course. You have already had some experience in woodcarving when you made your hand puppets. That experience will be very useful to you now that you are going to do a great deal more carving. Carving takes time and patience, so don't be anxious to get it all done quickly. It is far better to work carefully, because with care your marionette will move better, look better, and perform for you a long time without needing any serious repairs. Besides head, hands, and feet, you will have to carve a torso, arms with elbow joints, and legs with knee joints. When you are ready to start, have paper and pencil, wood, and tools always within reach. Make the customary and indispensable sketch of your marionette. Make your first working drawing without the costume—something like the illustration. From that sketch mark out the body or torso on a block of wood. For practical purposes, let's make our marionette two feet tall.

Start with the torso, which is the simplest of all parts to carve. Make it seven inches long and five inches across the shoulders. Put the block in your vise. Cut away the outline

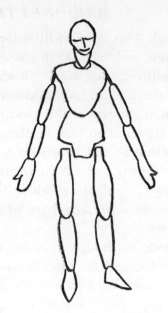

Holes for joints

A working sketch

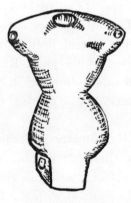

Finished torso

A WOODEN MARIONETTE

of the torso with saw and chisel. This done, drill holes for the attachment of the head, arms, and legs. Do this now, so you will avoid the danger of splitting your wood. To attach the head, drill a hole three-quarters of an inch in diameter and an inch and one-half deep at the top of the torso. For the arms drill holes about one-eighth of an inch in diameter at the ends of the shoulders. These should be drilled at an angle so that they pierce through at the back. Then, to attach the legs, drill another hole about an eighth of an inch in diameter through the base of the torso laterally. Now whittle down the torso to its finished form.

Make the legs twelve inches long. Each leg will be in three parts—the upper leg, the lower leg, and the foot. Make the upper leg six inches long, the lower leg five, and the foot one inch from heel to ankle, using a piece of wood one inch square. Drill a lateral one-eighth inch hole at one end of the upper legs to attach the torso. At the other end cut away half the thickness, about an inch, which will serve as one part of the knee joint. Then make the same cut at the top of the lower leg. Fit both pieces together, clamp them in your vise, and drill a lateral hole through the middle, thereby making a "lapped" knee joint. Round off the edges and slip a cord through this hole which will bind both parts and form the flexible knee. Shape the legs to a proportionate thickness.

Using the same one-inch-square stick, mark out the feet, heel to heel, and carve them after your pattern. Saw them apart, whittle them into form, and join them to the ends of the lower legs, exactly as you did with the knee.

The construction of the arms is not very different from that of the legs. Using wood of the same thickness (one inch) make the upper arms three inches long, the forearm and hands (which can be of one piece) five inches. Drill a hole through

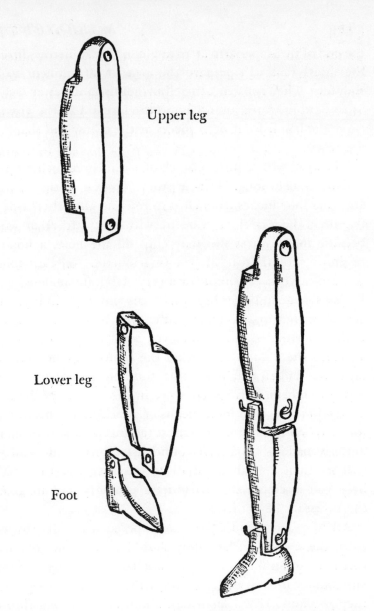

Upper leg

Lower leg

Foot

The leg assembled

A WOODEN LEG

the end of the upper arm at an angle so that it pierces through the sides. This will prepare the arm for attachment to the shoulder. Then construct the elbow joints in the same fashion as you did the knee joint. Clamp the forearm in the vise and carve the hand. Joint both pieces at the elbow and shape the entire arm.

The head will require a block of wood three inches square and five inches long. Draw a profile on one of the surfaces, allowing four inches from chin to top and the other inch for the neck. Be extremely careful with your chisel or knife, because the slightest slip may chip off the nose, a horrible beginning for the life of your marionette. Needless to say, you can carve a very simple or a very elaborate modeled head. Perhaps you had better begin with the simplest kind; you can get more imaginative after you've had more practice. Start with two rounded bumps for eyes, a ridge for the nose, and a slit for the mouth. Round off the bottom of the neck and taper the end so that it fits into the hole you drilled at the top of the torso. Drive a screw-eye in the bottom of the neck. This will serve as an ideal means of attaching the head to the torso. When this is done the most tedious part of your marionette is made—if you have found it tedious at all—and you will see then that all the drilling was necessary in order to help you assemble the marionette properly and to give it the necessary flexibility.

All the parts must be sandpapered carefully to give them the smooth surface they should have. Now comes the thrill of assembling your marionette and seeing it as the animate creature it is. First, insert the neck into its place in the torso and drive a small nail about an inch long through one side of the body so that it pierces the screw-eye at the end of the neck, crosses the hole, and comes through at the other side of the body. This attaches the head loosely enough

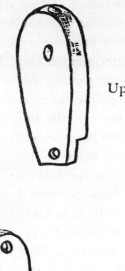

Upper arm

Lower arm and hand

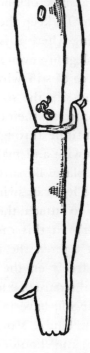

Arm assembled

A WOODEN ARM

to enable it to turn from side to side and up and down. Then drive two tiny screw-eyes just behind the top of the ears, tie a nylon string to them, and hang that much of the marionette where you can easily continue working. The two screw-eyes on the head are permanent parts of the mechanism.

Slip a heavy string through the holes at the top of each arm. When that comes through at the side, tie a knot and fasten it there with glue. Then pass the two loose ends at the top of the arms through the holes in the shoulder joints, and when they come through at the back, tie them together. Leave a slack of about an inch between the shoulder and the arm. To keep the arms in their proper places, tack down the string where it is knotted in the middle of the back.

The legs are even simpler to attach. All you need for these is a piece of stiff wire. Make a small loop at one end of the wire and slip the straight end first through the hole at the top of one leg, then through the hole at the base of the body and continue through the hole in the other leg. Cut away surplus wire and make another loop at this end to lock the legs in place. Be sure to adjust the two ends of the wire so that the legs can swing freely. You can use a bolt instead of a wire to attach the legs if you wish (this will make it stronger). In this case make certain it is the right length. Do not tighten the bolt. Leave it loose enough so the leg swings freely on the bolt, which acts as a pivot. The head of it will secure one leg section and the nut the other section.

So far you have provided only two screw-eyes by which to hang the figure. More will be necessary. Drive one screw-eye between the shoulder blades, one in each knee, and one in the back of each hand. These will be ample to string the marionette and make it walk, bow, move its hands, and turn its head. But before you string your marionette, he must be painted. Get out your show-card colors, which you will remember you used to paint your puppet, and get to work. Keep the joints free from paint; otherwise you may have trouble in making the figure move cleanly. When you have finished the painting, you will probably feel as pleased as Gepetto did when he finished carving and painting the eager-eyed Pinocchio. A costume will complete your creation and give him life, character, and motion.

You are in a colorful world of make-believe where everything is brighter and gayer. So just a covering will definitely be out of place. Let's consider the possibilities: a clown is rather ordinary. A pirate, a gypsy, a beggar? Still not picturesque enough. Our marionette is something special and very distinctive; he needs something bold and regal. How about a knight in full armor then? Perfect. Let's make him the most shining knight that ever rescued a fair damsel.

We'll need a tunic, cloak, and various pieces of body armor. First, cut out your patterns. Select your materials. Sew the tunic and cloak and try the tunic on the figure. The cloak will be more elegant and dashing if you line it with a silk of contrasting color (a black cloak lined with brilliant yellow is one suggestion).

Now comes the armor; if you're careful and follow directions you won't have too much trouble in making it. Your armor can be made either from thin sheet metal, such as shim brass, or, if this is too expensive or impractical, cardboard or buckram will do nicely and are easier to work with. The metal will look better and will clank gratifyingly, but cardboard or buckram can be made to resemble shiny armor— and, after all, it's all an illusion.

Anyway, whichever you decide upon, the making follows the same pattern. You need separate pieces for the breast, the back, the arms, the legs, the hips, the shield, and the helmet. Before cutting your material, it may be wise to experiment with paper patterns of all the pieces. Cut out the different parts from your experimental patterns, shape them, and sew them into their proper form. Link the breast and hip pieces together with narrow tape. If you're working with cardboard or buckram you can give the armor a rich metallic appearance by painting the parts with a prepared bronze mixture. This will also strengthen the material. Allow the paint to dry and then you are ready to help your marionette try on his armor. If all is well, he may graciously permit you to be his squire.

Begin with the leg pieces. Secure them in place with a tape lacing at the back. Sew the arm pieces in place next. Then put the back and breast pieces in place over the tunic and sew them together. Fit the helmet on the head and tack it at the back.

You might have chosen shim brass instead of cardboard and, as we've said, the patterns are identical. But you will need a few additional tools and perhaps a bit more patience. The extra tools are a pair of metal-cutting shears, a small nail punch, pliers, and aluminum rivets. Cut out all your pieces, shape them, and then rivet them in form. For example, take the breast plate: cut the slit from the neck to the center, lap the cut to shape the breast plate, punch a hole through the lapped pieces, slip a rivet through the hole as you would a nail, clip off the excess length of the rivet with your pliers, and hammer it down until it spreads and secures the two pieces. Beat the rivets on a metal base.

Punch parallel holes in the breast and hip pieces and link them together with leather thongs, knotted at both ends. Then punch holes along the sides and shoulders of both breast and back pieces. Put them in place on the marionette and use a thin wire with which to lace them in place. Rivet the helmet into form with two rivets at the back and slip it

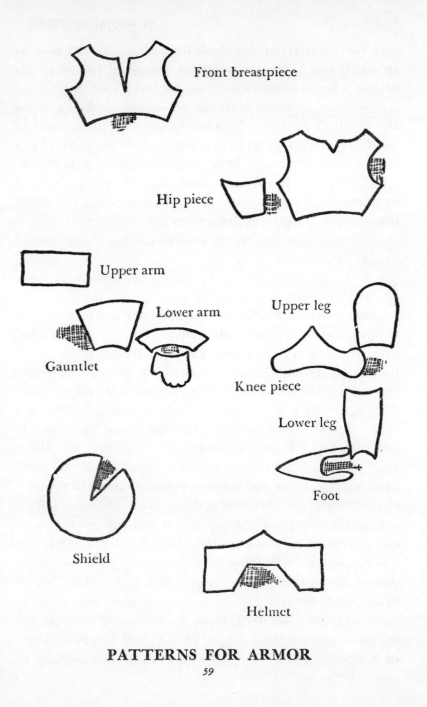

Front breastpiece

Hip piece

Upper arm

Lower arm

Upper leg

Gauntlet

Knee piece

Lower leg

Foot

Shield

Helmet

PATTERNS FOR ARMOR

over the head. Hang the cloak from the shoulders and, as an added touch, give your knight a colorful plume in his helmet, a sword in one hand, and a shield in the other.

Punch a hole through the center of your knight's shield and nail it to the back of his hand. A sword can be made of wood and painted silver. Drill a hole through the hilt end and force a stiff wire into it. Drill a hole through the hand, slip the wire through the hilt and hand, and then bend it around to secure the bottom of the hand. This prevents the sword from slipping. Now you have a knight ready to sally forth to challenge any dragon to mortal combat—after you've strung him.

Two-rod control

Now that you are ready to string the marionette, you need to know a method of control. A simple two-rod control, used with the famous Sicilian marionettes, consists merely of a thin metal rod attached to the head, another to the sword hand, and a string to the shield. If you care to try this method, drive a screw-eye at the top of the head, hook the end of a thin rod, one or two feet long, through it and bend the top end into a crook. Hook the other end of the rod, about twice as long, around the wire hilt of the sword between the hand and the blade and make a round loop at the top end of this rod so that you can slip the head rod through it.

Fasten a string to the top of the shield and tie the other end to the top of the head rod. That is all you need, and this is perhaps the simplest of all methods for the manipulation of marionettes which are operated from above. No leg strings are needed.

To work this two-rod control, you hold the crook of the head rod in your left hand and the rod of the sword hand in your right hand. For a walking position raise and lower

Parts of breastplate

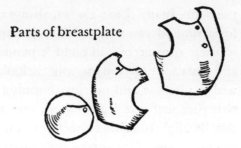

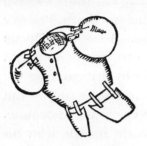

Breastplate complete

Arm pieces

Leg pieces

Helmet

Shield

ARMOR ASSEMBLED

the figure in quick succession, always moving the arms slightly forward, and you will see that the legs swing back and forth of their own accord like clock pendulums. A little practice and you can make the marionette look like he's really walking with a purpose and not just flopping up and down. Practice swinging first one leg forward, and then the other. You do this by slightly raising the figure and turning your wrist at the same time. Now make it gesticulate by maneuvering the rod attached to the sword hand. You will see that you can produce very effective gestures that are vigorous and definite. You can make your knight slap his shield smartly with his sword and deal energetic blows at his adversary, either with the point of his sword or the blade. You raise the shield over his head by pulling the strings with your little finger of the hand which is handling the head rod. If you make and operate two marionettes like this you can stage the most thrilling and realistic duel ever seen on any stage.

String control

Your marionette is also adapted for a more complicated control system which you may like to try. This type involves several strings, but no rods. If you would like to go on, make the control first. This is made of wood and is of two parts: the main part, to which the head, back, and hands are attached; and a supplementary plain stick which controls the legs. The main part is made of two sticks crossed to form a "T."

A very practical method of attaching strings to a control is by making saw slits about an inch long in the places where the strings are to be tied. Through these the strings are slipped and wound without the necessity of making knots. For stringing, use a thin fishing line or a very heavy linen thread. You have seven different places to attach strings on a mario-

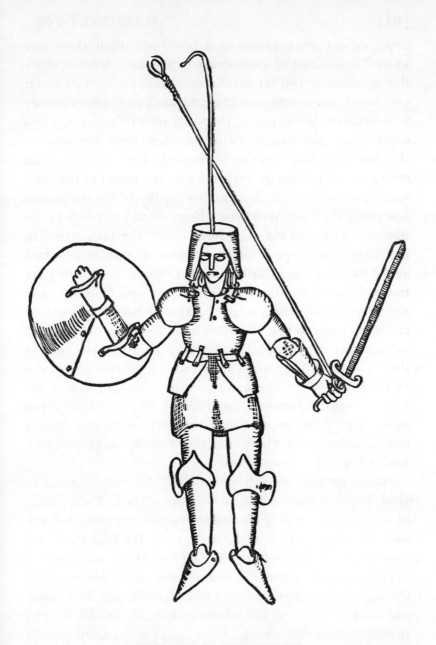

TWO-ROD CONTROL

nette. So cut seven pieces of string, each about three feet long. Tie one end of each string to the little screw-eyes on the marionette: two on the head, one at the back, one on each hand, and one on each knee. Fasten a short heavy leather strap securely to the top of the main control where the two sticks cross, and hang it about four feet from the floor so that the crosspiece remains horizontal. Take the two head strings and slip them through the slits at the end of the horizontal piece and adjust them so that the feet of the marionette just touch the floor. Wind the strings around the ends of the stick and fasten in the slits. Next attach the back string to the perpendicular piece of the control, so that it is as taut as the strings fastened to the head. Consult the drawing for the position of the slits on the control. Now take the hand strings and attach them to the horizontal bar of the control, adjusting them so that the arms hang limply to the sides of the figure. Lastly, attach the two knee strings to the ends of the separate stick, adjusted long enough for the leg control to reach the top of the main control without bending the knees of your marionette. To finish off, you might put a peg at the top of the main control from which the leg control can be secured when not in use. That completes the stringing. Let's try working your figure.

Have him take his first steps. Hold the main control in your left hand and the foot piece in your right. The walking of a marionette strung on such a control requires that you move both your hands at the same time. It's important that every muscle of your entire body be brought into active play to give the illusion of a fluid, smooth, unbroken rhythm. With the right hand you tilt the foot piece first up and then down, and with the left hand you advance the main control, turning it slightly from side to side. Practice these two simultaneous movements until your marionette has learned to walk well.

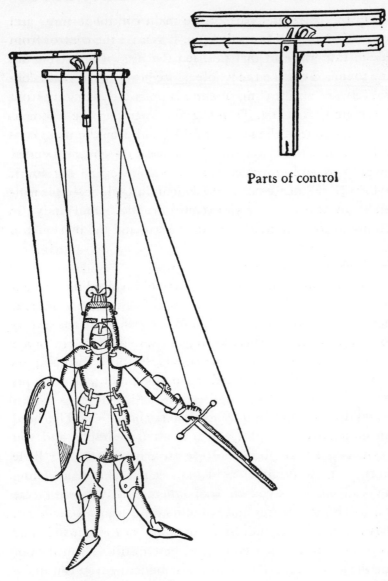

Parts of control

Marionette on control

STRING CONTROL

Tip the horizontal part of the main control forward and the marionette will bow his head. If you tip the control from side to side while in that position the head will shake from side to side. To make the whole figure bow, tip the main control forward until the marionette is practically hanging from the single back string. To make him kneel, tip the foot control so that one of the knees is raised and drop the main control so that the marionette kneels gallantly on one bended knee. Expressive movements, such as pointing, sitting down, saying yes and no, weeping and dancing, all will be simple matters if you will examine your control carefully and study the relationship of the strings to the control and the marionette.

Papier-maché marionettes

You now know a number of principles involved in the making of marionettes. Perhaps you would like to go further and make one out of papier-maché. This type of figure has several distinct advantages, such as lightness, mobility, etc. Even without a rudimentary knowledge of sculpture, which goes into the making of this type, come along and pick up hints as we start on this type of figure.

You'll need modeling clay, plaster, and paper. The head can be made quite light, which is often desirable, and you can make many duplicates of the same head with very little effort after the original mold has been made. In modeling the head and torso, you can shape them exactly as you please and watch the features and contours grow under your hand. It is a building-up process as opposed to the cutting-away process of the wooden type. And better still, if you do not like the appearance of what you are modeling, you can easily change it without spoiling it.

Let us start with the head. There are two kinds of clay you can use. One is ordinary clay and the other a composition

For walking

For bowing

For sitting down

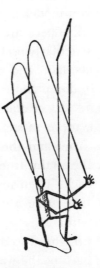

For kneeling

POSITIONS OF CONTROL

called plasteline. Plasteline is more expensive, but as it mixes with oil it is always ready for modeling, while with clay you must keep it moistened with water to retain a modeling consistency. However, either is good for the purpose at hand, and you'll get the same finished results if you follow directions carefully.

If you decide to work with clay, be sure it has no lumps. If it is not smooth enough, knead it thoroughly, adding a little water as you do. A stick with a knob on the end will serve as an armature upon which to build your clay head. Grip the end of the stick in the vise and build your clay head on the knob. Keep adding clay, bit by bit, until you have shaped what looks like a head. Watch the proportions carefully so that you do not model it too large or too small. If your marionette is to be two feet tall, make the head about four inches long from chin to top. Always remember that whatever you model in clay will show in the finished papier-maché head. There are regular inexpensive modeling tools that are particularly useful for details such as the mouth, eyes, nostrils, ears, hair, and wrinkles. Always keep the clay model wrapped in damp cloths when not working on it, so that the clay does not dry or crack in the interim. When the modeling is finished, the next step is to make the plaster mold in two parts, the front and the back.

First make a faint line around the head, marking the front from the back. Then make a roll of clay, flatten it, and cut it into a long strip about an inch wide and half an inch thick. Place this strip of clay edgewise along the division line marked on the head so that it forms a wall. Put lumps of clay along the back of the wall like buttresses. You must first cast the front half of the head. To prepare for casting, settle the back of the head in a coil of clay laid on a flat surface. Then take two or three sheets of heavy wrapping paper six or eight

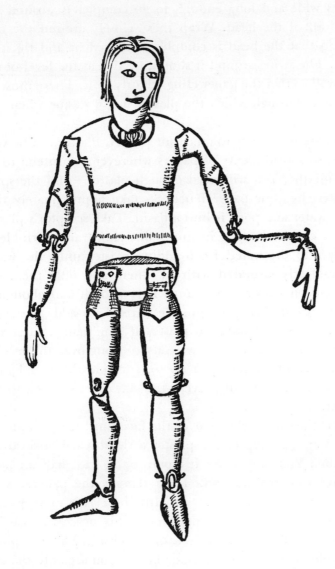

PAPIER-MACHÉ MARIONETTE

inches wide and long enough to go completely around the clay wall of the head. Wrap these closely around the clay wall so that the head is completely fenced in and tie it in place. The string around it should be tied at the level of the clay wall so that the paper clings tightly to it. There must be no spaces through which the plaster might escape when you start casting.

You are now ready to mix your plaster. Plaster can be very messy, so spread plenty of papers wherever you intend to do your mixing. You will need enough plaster to fill the space enclosed by your paper fence. So take approximately that much water and pour it into a basin. Take sculptor's plaster (which can be bought in any paint shop) and sprinkle it slowly into the water. Keep adding plaster until the water is completely saturated with it. Then, and only then, stir the solution with a spoon until it is smooth and about the consistency of heavy cream. Be careful to add plaster to water. Never add water to plaster if you want a successful mixture. The plaster is now ready to pour over the face in the casing. But before you do so, sprinkle the face lightly with water, which will prevent the clay from sticking to the plaster.

Pour the plaster slowly over the face until it is completely buried and the top of the plaster at least a half-inch above the nose. You must leave it alone for at least half an hour to have it thoroughly set. Then remove the paper casing, turn the whole thing over, and lift the clay wall very carefully out of its plaster bed. Repeat this process in casting the back of the head, paper casing and all. This completes the mold. Wait at least an hour before you separate the two halves of the plaster mold.

Then tap gently all around the joint with a wooden mallet; pull the two halves apart. If you run into difficulty in separat-

The armature

Clay head on armature

Dividing clay wall in place

MODELING A CLAY HEAD

ing the parts, pry a metal blade into the slit and slowly and gently force them open. Remove the clay and you have the negative, or mold, of the original clay head. From that you make your papier-maché copies. The same steps followed in making the mold apply for the torso, legs, or arms of papier-maché. It's really fun to make this kind of marionettes. You can, if you wish, make the head and torso all in one piece and cut them apart after they are finished in paper.

Now for your copies. You need paper and paste. You can use almost any kind of paper, but the best—by test—is a water-color paper. Soak it in water, crush it in your hands and wring it dry as you can. Mix some wallpaper paste (available at any paint shop) with water and a little glue until it has the consistency of a thick cream sauce. Tear (don't cut) your paper in small pieces and lay them carefully in the mold. Do the back of the head first; it's simpler. Use no paste with the first layer. Beginning with the second layer, smear each piece of paper on both sides with your prepared paste. Four or five layers of paper will give you a substantial mask. If you want a head to be particularly durable, use alternate layers of paper and cloth. Press each piece of paper in very carefully so that none of the modeling is lost. When the last layer is pressed, set the molds aside to dry. They may take up to two days to dry thoroughly; don't be impatient—wait. You can tell pretty well if they are dry enough—then the paper masks comes out of their molds without effort. Otherwise they might pull out of shape. Trim off the superfluous edges.

Fasten two little wire loops in the back half of the mold, one at either side, about where the back of the ear is. Push the wire loops through from the inside and make them fast there with paper and paste. Also take a round block of wood the thickness of the neck and glue it in the front half of the

Paper being laid in mold

Back half of mask

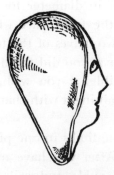

Front half of mask

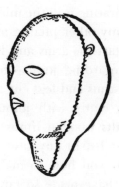

Halves joined

MAKING A PAPIER-MACHÉ HEAD

neck. Then fit the front and back halves of the head together
and bind with paper and paste. Paste down all loose pieces
on the surface and lay aside the head to dry. When the head
is completely dry, compare its weight to a wooden head;
you'll be amazed and pleased at how much lighter the paper
head is, and, subsequently so much easier to work with.

Make the torso in exactly the same fashion: take the two
halves of it and equip them with the necessary mechanism
for assembling and stringing by putting a wire loop in the
middle of the back between the shoulders (this will serve to
hang the marionette). Before we go any further, the torso
must be reinforced with wood blocks. You do this by insert-
ing inside the puppet's body (shape if necessary to conform
with the shape of the body) a strip of wood an inch thick
from shoulder to shoulder. Drill a hole in the center of the
puppet's back three-fourths of an inch in diameter for the
neck. Fit another block of wood in the front part where
the legs are to be attached. Now the two halves of the torso
are joined together in the same manner as you did the head.

You can make the torso more flexible, if you wish, by
separating it in the middle and then rejoining it with chamois
or any other pliable material.

Start the arms and legs by making the limbs in one piece,
disregarding joints—for the present. After you have made
the arms and legs cut them at the knee, ankle, and wrist and
now equip with joints. However, for the most satisfactory
results wooden limbs are best in the long run. The joints
must be, in any case, made of wood. The illustration will
show you how to make a different kind of joint from any
you have made so far. It is like a loose mortise and tenon
joint, one fitting into the other and connected by a wire pin
through holes drilled in both pieces.

To make a pair of legs with joints of this kind, take a

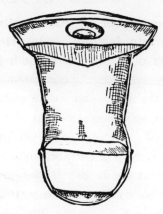

Half of torso equipped
with wood blocks

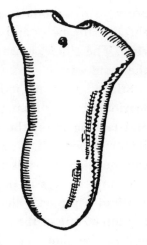

Two halves joined

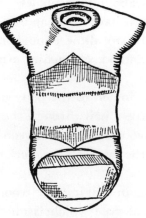

Chamois joint for
flexible torso

PAPIER-MACHÉ TORSO

round stick of soft wood, the diameter being not less than the thickest part of the leg. Cut four lengths, two for the upper and two for the lower part of the legs. Put each in the vise and drill small holes through them about one-half inch thick from the ends where the knee and ankle joints are to be. Then, for the knee joint, scoop out the end of the upper leg and cut down the end of the lower leg until you are able to fit one into the other. Slip a connecting wire through the holes and make it bend freely before you proceed. The elbow, wrist, and ankle joints are made exactly in the same way.

Still another method of attaching arms and legs to your marionette is by taking a strip of muslin, three inches long, and tacking it on the top of the leg, letting it project an inch and one-half. Now join the legs to the body by nailing the muslin strip ends to the wood at the base of the torso, allowing the legs to dangle loosely.

Wind a piece of chamois about four inches long around the top of one of the arms you have made and glue it to the end of the shoulder. Be sure to allow enough chamois to ensure flexible joints. This method of attaching arms and legs is very practical in all cases.

The papier-maché head is joined to the body in the same way as the wooden one. Drive a nail through the torso that will pierce the hole in the wooden block between the shoulders and the screw-eye at the base of the neck, as clearly shown in the illustration.

If you are having trouble in making the wooden joints, you can use another practical type which is much simpler, particularly in the case of the ankles, wrists, and elbows. Take a wrist joint for instance. Drive a screw-eye in the end of the hand and one in the end of the forearm and lock one screw-eye in the other so that it forms a link. Then cover

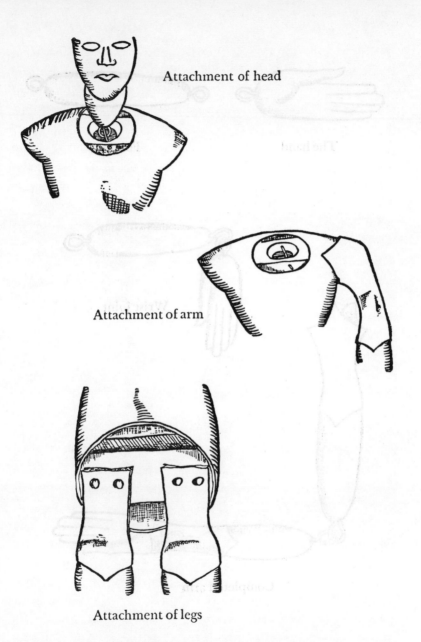

Attachment of head

Attachment of arm

Attachment of legs

ASSEMBLING THE PARTS

77

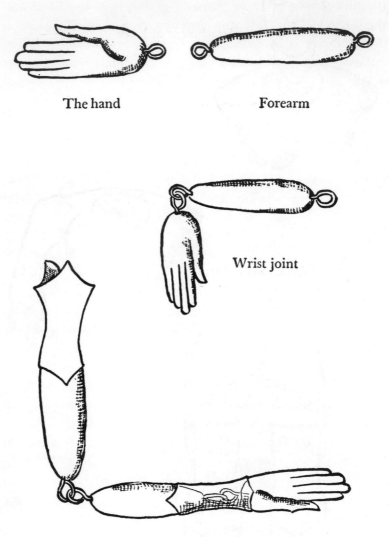

The hand   Forearm

Wrist joint

Completed arm

USING SCREW-EYES

the link with a piece of chamois, gluing it to the hand and the forearm. Don't use this kind of a joint at the knee unless the character is an eccentric one.

Before going on to the painting of your marionette, let us quickly look at still another type of torso which is quicker to make and much less complicated. This torso is made of cloth, stuffed and covered with paper and paste, so that when it is finished it resembles a papier-maché product. It looks like one, all right, but it won't hold up as long; it will do for rarely used characters, however. To make this type, cut your patterns, as usual, of the front and back, each two pieces, and then sew them together as the drawing shows. Leave openings at the armholes, neck, and bottom. Turn it and stuff it tightly with cotton. This stuffing is temporary, but needed to hold the form for papering. Smear with paste and then cover the entire surface with three layers of paper and paste. Lay it aside until thoroughly dry. Remove the stuffing and equip it with the mechanism for assembling and stringing as already outlined.

Making a marionette of plastic wood

Then there is the durable and handsome marionette you can make of plastic wood. This type has several advantages over the others you have already made. It is much lighter than ordinary wood, stronger than papier-maché, and dries faster. The material is fairly inexpensive and readily obtainable at your paint or art shop. It is fairly easy to use, and if you care to try it—follow directions carefully!

For example, let's start with the head. Set up your mold exactly in the same fashion as you did with the papier-maché model. Then get a pail, or a pan, that is deep enough to completely submerge your plaster mold. Fill it with water and sink your complete mold in it—entirely covered—until the air bubbles stop rising to the surface. Then remove one-half of the mold and place it on your work table. Now roll a small handful of plastic wood in your palm until it is firm. (Always keep your hands wet while working with plastic wood to keep it from sticking to you.) Lay this roll of plastic wood on your plaster mold and press it to an approximate thickness of one-eighth inch. Continue adding rolls of plastic wood until the complete surface of the mold is covered evenly. The important thing to keep in mind is to lay on the plastic wood as level with the edge of the mold as possible. Don't try to press it over the edge of the mold. The sharper the break around the edge, the easier it will be to fit to the other half of the head later.

After you have finished filling one-half of the mold, wrap it in a wet rag to keep it from drying, and put it aside in a safe place. Then take out of the pail the other half of the mold and cover the inside with plastic wood, going through exactly the same process as you did with the first half. Make sure you spread the plastic wood evenly. When this is done you're ready to join the two halves together. The best way to tie the two halves together is to use a strong piece of string. Wet the string to prevent shrinking. To join the halves together, roll enough strips of plastic wood about the thickness of an ordinary lead pencil and line them along the seam where the two halves meet inside the mold. Press lightly with a modeling stick or any round-edged tool. While doing this, apply a coat of commercial lacquer thinner along the seams to keep the plastic wood soft.

When the seams have been joined together with your rolled strips of plastic wood, plunge the entire mold in water and soak it for a half-hour. When the time is up, loosen the string, *always keeping the whole mold in water.* Then slowly ease the plastic wood around the edges and gently, very gently,

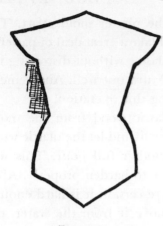

Pattern

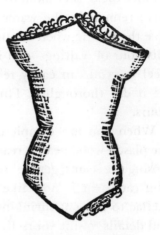

Cloth torso stuffed

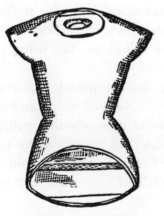

Torso papered, stuffing
removed and completed

STUFFED-CLOTH TORSO

start prying the two halves of the plaster mold apart. The plastic wood is still soft and it will take a great deal of patience and care to remove it from the plaster without distorting the modeling. Be careful and all will turn out well. And remember—it is still under water during this operation.

After you've separated the plastic wood from the mold, remove the plaster mold from the pail and let the plastic wood form remain in the water for another full hour. This will give the plastic wood enough time to harden properly. After this hour of waiting—and if you're certain it is hard enough (feel it—you can easily tell) remove it from the water and let it dry thoroughly. This will take from eight to twelve hours.

When you are completely satisfied it is thoroughly dry, the plastic wood head is ready to receive additional treatment: closing the seams, general retouching, and final sandpapering. You can treat it now like ordinary wood. Apply a coat of shellac to prevent shrinking and when dry, paint in features and details to suit yourself. Other parts of the body are made by following the papier-maché technique, but using plastic wood.

Let's get back to painting our completed papier-maché marionette. Up to this point we have used only water colors. Let's go a step further and use a more durable paint that is mixed with oil and turpentine. Oil paints can be bought in any art supply shop and they come in any color you fancy. You will also need a small bottle of turpentine and one of dryer.

Dilute the color you choose with turpentine and add a drop or two of dryer which will hasten the process of drying. Oil colors will strengthen your masks and make them waterproof. For that reason it is wise to give not only the head, but all parts, a coat of paint.

By this time you ought to be pretty good at designing and making costumes to fit your figures. You have made a suit of armor and also a Pierrot costume. Whatever you decide to dress this papier-maché marionette in, follow the general rules that guided you with the other two. Above all keep the joints flexible; do not design a costume that will hamper easy movement at the joints. Much of the success of a marionette's performance depends largely on how well he responds to the manipulator's control. If the limbs are stiffened by the costume, he will not walk and make gestures as gracefully as you would like him to do. Not only must you make your marionette well-balanced and flexible, but it is important to see that the costume destroys none of this and is in reality a help and a part of the construction.

We've brought you this far in making various types of marionettes, but it is also good to experiment with new materials. Why not try foam rubber in making a torso for one of your marionettes?

Carve from wood a shoulder-piece and a torso base exactly as you did with your wooden marionette, using the same measurements. Glue a rectangular one-inch thick piece of foam rubber to the top of the shoulders to the bottom of the torso—both front and back. This is all that is necessary to firmly connect the two pieces. When dry, take a pair of scissors and cut your foam rubber to the shape you want the torso to be. If you want certain parts thicker, add more rubber foam to those parts, using rubber cement to attach it. You can further secure it by driving a few very small nails through the rubber into the wooden shoulder frame and torso piece.

Using foam rubber has many advantages. You can dress the figure directly without a lot of sewing and fitting. You don't have to mold a papier-maché, canvas, or cotton body. It is much lighter than any other material. It never lumps or goes out of shape and it is much more durable than most other materials. You can also shape legs and arms with foam rubber.

Making them act

You know how to equip your marionette with more than one type of control—either rods or strings; both are good and professionally acceptable.

The string control allows you to use as many strings as you feel necessary to make your marionette perform any special stunt and movement. If you find you are happiest working with papier-maché marionettes, this type of control will be about the best you can use. There are other more complicated forms of string control in use, but they sometimes take up unnecessary space, hamper the manipulator, and the results are about the same.

There are no set rules about the number of strings that a marionette should have except, perhaps, that it should have as few as possible. In the excitement and motion of giving a performance, too many strings are much more likely to get tangled than too few. With practice you can make your marionette obey, using the minimum number of strings.

It will be only through simple direct means that you will get the best results—from the construction of the marionette right through to the final performance. It cannot be overstressed that simplicity is the best policy. Don't get too complicated. You're giving an original performance, not imitating a magician's obvious tricks. For instance, it is not necessary for a marionette's mouth to open and close and his eyes to roll to give your audience the impression he's acting—and ham acting at that. Depend upon the modeling, the painting, and the dressing for realistic expression. If you plan it out carefully and take your time, the marionette will seem to change its expression and move every feature as he plays out his role—subtly and effectively.

The Sicilian marionettes were among the most primitive of professional performers. You will remember that they were manipulated by only two rods and one string. Their faces were, in repose, like stone images and yet when they were put on the stage they instantly became alive—registering every shade of human emotion, from deep melancholy to frantic rage. In all their productions the wise Sicilians emphasized only the important things. Their gestures were few but vigorous and to the point. If you're seriously interested in doing good work you can learn a great deal from the people who discovered long ago the secret of simplicity.

There is a good way of manipulating a marionette and a bad way; you have probably seen both and possibly will do both—until you learn better. Because a marionette is supposed to be talking, it is not necessary to keep him jiggling nervously so that it looks to the audience as if he had a bad case of St. Vitus' dance. Movements and gestures should be well thought out and the fewer the better. It is only then that they count and register with the audience—young children included. Jerky insignificant gestures can spoil the meaning of a speech and the mood of a scene and annoy the audience to the point where they're not watching or listening. The part of the manipulator can best be compared to that of an actor. He must sense the meaning of the lines and not only speak them well but translate them into the marionette's movements so that the lines do not mean one thing and the movements another. You cannot afford to relax your attention from the marionette you are manipulating—or endowing with life. You can't afford to forget your lines. The marionette can be compared to a musical instrument.

The musician cannot possibly play one melody and think of another. You must, by the same token, concentrate on the marionette you are working. Then, and only then, will he transfer your sincere efforts into dramatic life of his own and vibrantly communicate them to an attentive, eager, appreciative audience.

The marionettes you have made are not the final chapter. These are fine but ready-made, and while they're fun to make and fun to work with, they're still not yours. If you've been successful with these models and have caught something of their enchantment, you're ready to try ideas of your own. When you make another marionette, add something new to him. Make him just a little different. You can make marionettes any size you want—from twelve inches to twelve feet high.

The stage

Marionettes, like actors, need a stage to perform on. In fact, they need a stage even more than actors do; it is the only world upon which they can really live. Marionettes have something to do only when they are on the stage. The only other alternative they have is to hang in a closet. Anyway, you didn't make the marionettes so that they could hang around a closet—so, let's discuss the making of a stage.

From the audience's point of view a stage for marionettes looks very much like a stage for puppets. Unfortunately, it isn't so. They are very different in construction. Puppets, of course, are manipulated from below the stage, while marionettes are worked with strings from above the stage. In a marionette theatre the position of the manipulator is such that he looks down on the marionettes to see how they are behaving. This position calls for an elevated structure directly behind the backdrop. The top of the backdrop is the level

IMPROVISED MARIONETTE THEATRE

over which you lean to work the figures on the stage below. It also forms a wall which hides your legs from the audience.

Before you start building, read each paragraph carefully.

There are several different types of stages you can build. Let's start with the easiest. You can improvise a simple marionette stage out of two soap boxes, two chairs, some drapery, and the nearest doorway. With the doorway you have a serviceable proscenium. Nail the soap boxes together and place them on the floor across the bottom of the doorway. (Choose a doorway through which there isn't too much traffic.) You now have a stage floor upon which your marionettes can perform, so cut two sticks of wood, each about three feet long, and nail them upright, one at each end toward the rear of the soap boxes, and nail another strip of thin wood across the top of these two. This framework will serve to hang your back scene from. Behind all this place your chairs. Being a little bit higher than the soap boxes, these will serve as a convenient level for you to stand on. Tack some drapery across the top of the doorway so that it reaches down to about two and one-half feet from the stage floor. This will form the top of your proscenium and will also hide you from the audience.

The stage curtain itself will reach from the point where your drapery stops to the stage floor. If you will turn back to the chapter on puppets you will find a detailed description showing exactly how to rig such a curtain. It means sewing rings at one end and slipping them through a wire stretched across the proscenium, the curtains being made to open and close by pulling strings systematically arranged.

One floor or desk lamp on each side of the stage, close to the proscenium curtain so that the faces of the marionettes get the full benefit of the light, will give you ample lighting effects. With this much equipment, which costs you very little effort and practically no expense, you can conduct a complete marionette show.

A little practical advice, before we continue. When you are ready to work the marionettes, stand on the chairs behind the backdrop and walk the marionettes on the stage floor, using the support of your stage setting as a rest for your arms. The two sides of your stage, you will notice, are clear and open for the marionettes to enter and exit. You will also need some contraption to hang them on when they are waiting for their cues. A hatrack, if you can get one, is ideal for hanging your marionettes. Otherwise, rig up any sort of a temporary screen behind the scenes within easy reaching distance, and make wire hooks shaped like an "S," one end of which hooks over the top of the screen or onto the hatrack.

In this simple structure you have used the essential principles that go into the making of a marionette theatre. It's far from being professional, and if you feel it's too much of a makeshift and would like to try constructing a fairly complicated stage, you'll see it's not prohibitively difficult: it will probably require a few days' hard work, which you will enjoy.

Let's start with the "bridge," which is the name given to that section where the manipulators stand while working the marionettes. To make this, get two ordinary stepladders three feet high, stand them five feet apart and lay a wide plank on top of them. Screw the plank down to the top of the ladders. Then reinforce the structure with braces three inches wide and one inch thick, across both ladders. To prevent the plank from sagging in the middle, put the same kind of braces underneath it on both sides, reaching from ladder to ladder. So much for the actual bridge. The next thing to make is a railing at the front and at the back of it. The one at the front will serve as a rest to lean over, as well as a place to hang your backdrop. The one at the back is a useful and handy place to hang your marionettes when they are not being used on the stage. It also will guard you from falling off. Use the same kind of strip lumber for the railings you used for the braces below, three inches wide by one inch thick. For the uprights supporting the railing, cut five strips three feet long and screw them vertically to the bridgework. Two go in the front and three in the back, placed several feet apart. Cut two more pieces six feet long and screw them fast across the uprights. When they are finished, these rails should be at least two and one-half to three feet from the floor of the bridge. Make certain that your bridge is very steady; and before you go any further, stand on it and shake it—if it's still standing, you've done a good workmanlike job. If it's the least bit shaky, brace the rails by screwing diagonal pieces from the top of the rail to the bridge floor. Of course, the rest of the structure, when built and assembled, will help steady your bridge.

The next thing to build is the stage floor upon which your marionettes are to perform. Make this about eighteen inches below the bridge floor and about the same distance from the ground. Construct the foundation of the floor first, which is a rectangular structure, six and one-half feet long by three feet wide, using a three-inch wide strip of lumber. Join these strips endwise as shown in the illustration. This will prevent sagging. Make marks eighteen inches from the ground on the two stepladders and nail or bolt the long side of this floor framework to both ladders. Prop up the other side until you are ready to nail the front of the theatre to it, which is your next step.

The front of the theatre which you are constructing contains the proscenium opening and acts also as a wall between the audience and you. With that end in view, it must be made high enough and wide enough for sufficient conceal-

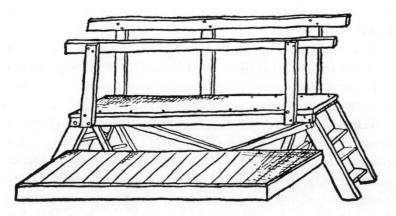

Framework for floor

Floor attached to bridge

THE STAGE FLOOR
91

ment. If the bridge on top of the stepladders is three feet from the ground, the top of the theatre should be six feet above that, making it nine feet from the ground altogether; with the length of the bridge being six feet, the width of your theatre front should be no less than eight feet.

In making the proscenium, the first thing you must do is to build a framework, using the same lumber as you did for the framework of your stage floor. Cut two strips nine feet long, one strip eight feet long, and two strips five feet long, the latter being for your proscenium opening. Put these pieces together as you see them in the illustration; the two nine-foot strips are the uprights, the two five-foot strips the top and bottom of the proscenium opening, and the eight-foot strip the extreme top of your structure. First nail the top and bottom proscenium pieces between the two uprights. The bottom crosspiece should be eighteen inches from the ground, and the top crosspiece four and one-half feet from the ground, which will give you a proscenium opening three feet high and five feet wide. Nail or bolt the top crosspiece in place. Insert diagonal braces at the bottom and top and you have the front framework of your theatre.

When this framework is satisfactorily completed, you are ready to join it to the rest of the structure. The lower cross-piece, which is the bottom of the proscenium, should register with the stage floor. Fit the front framework against the stage floor frame and nail it there. You may find it necessary to brace the large front framework in several places. In that case you might add extra braces tying the bottom of the uprights to the stepladders—that will be sufficient to make the entire front rigid. For further strength the top can be braced with two pieces at right angles, tying the top of the front frame to the back rail of the bridge. That adds solidity to your whole equipment and in no way interferes with the

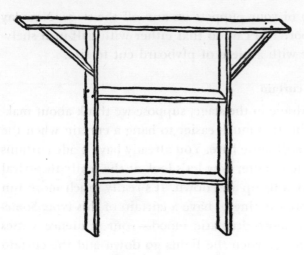

The Framework

Framework attached to floor

THE PROSCENIUM

manipulation of your puppets on and off the stage. Now lay your stage floor. You can do that either with half-inch shelving planks or with a piece of plyboard cut to size.

Making a roll curtain

Before we drape in the stage, suppose we think about making the curtain. It is much easier to hang a curtain when the framework is still quite bare. You already have made curtains that part in the middle; now let's look at the really theatrical kind, one that rolls up and down. It's really much more fun and much more exciting to have a curtain of this type. Somehow it adds a more dramatic mood—your audience senses momentous things when the lights go down and the curtain slowly rises. As a matter of fact, this is one of the most enchanting moments in the theatre. If your play is lively, make your curtain go up like a streak of lightning, and you can add emphasis to a dramatic finale by dropping your curtain like a thunderbolt. Make the audience feel that when the curtain flies down they have seen something really special and definite. A really fine curtain resembles the gestures of an old-fashioned actor: it makes its exit and its entrance with as much gusto and much the same exaggerated air.

But, like everything else, there are two schools of thought on this subject. So, before we tackle the roll curtain, let's look at the arguments pro and con. The part-in-the-middle curtain is simpler to make and more reliable. The roll type does get snagged and it requires constant care. Before each performance you must check the spools, see that the strings aren't fouled, and make sure it rolls evenly. You rarely have trouble with the simpler type; like the proverbial brook, it runs quietly forever.

We confess a preference to the more dramatic roll curtain. However, the choice is entirely up to you. But, if you possess an adventurous and inquiring turn of mind, let's proceed with the practical side of the roll-type curtain, since you already know how to make the other type. For the proscenium you have just built, you need a piece of cloth six and one-half feet long by four feet wide for your curtain. You need a bottom pole to make your curtain hang solidly: either a heavy, rounded stick or, if you can get it without too much trouble, a piece of brass tubing an inch in diameter will do. Make your pole six feet long. Attach a large wooden spool to either end. Fasten the spools solidly so that they do not spin around the pole. Glue one of the long edges of the curtain cloth at right angles to the pole. Then run the pole until the cloth is completely used up. Make sure it does not go off at an angle.

Then tack the other long edge of the cloth to a stick, six and one-half feet long. This done, nail the stick on the inside of the front frame two inches above the top proscenium strip,

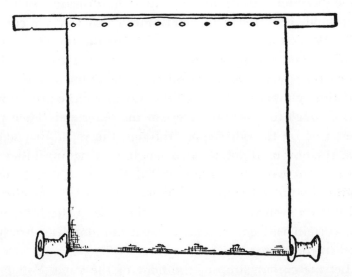

CURTAIN ATTACHED TO POLE AND STICK

and allow the curtain to roll down to the stage floor. You will notice that a certain portion of the lower part of the curtain is still rolled around the pole, which is as it should be.

Make marks at each end of the strip of wood at the top of the curtain so that they are on a line with the center of the two spools attached to the bottom pole. Drive one screw-eye at the mark you have made at one end of the stick and two screw-eyes a few inches apart at the mark at the other end of the stick. Then take two heavy mason lines (which you can get at any hardware store) about twenty feet long, and wax them well with paraffin. Fasten one end at one spool to the right and one end to the spool at the left. The ends of the strings must be secured with glue and a tack so that there is no chance of their slipping. The next step is to roll your curtain tight to the very top of the proscenium. Then wind the strings half a dozen times around their respective spools. Make sure in winding the strings that they both go in the same direction. Also remember that the direction in which you wind the strings will determine which way the curtain rolls. While the curtain is still rolled at the top of the pro-scenium and the strings wound around the spools a half dozen times, pass the string on the side of the single screw-eye, through that screw-eye all the way across the proscenium and through the outer screw-eye at the other end. Then pass the string on the other spool through the remaining screw-eye. You now must pull the two dangling strings until they are evenly taut with the curtain rolled tightly. Then, holding both strings together, release them slowly so that the curtain rolls down evenly. The weight of the pole at the bottom of the curtain will ensure that the curtain unrolls when you slacken the strings.

Let the curtain drop to the floor of the stage. You must now fix the two strings so that they will always pull evenly when you want to raise or lower the curtain. To do this get a metal ring and tie both strings to it as close to the two screw-eyes at the top of the curtain as you can get it, while the curtain is still fully lowered. You'll find this works very nicely, and saves a lot of time adjusting the strings every time you pull the curtain. To keep your curtain up during a performance, attach a hook to some convenient point of the framework and slip your ring onto it. It might be a good idea to tie a second ring to your curtain strings about two feet below the first; this will help you handle the curtain rigging more easily when you want to raise it.

Your curtain will work better if it is painted. Paint gives it just the right amount of stiffening it needs to prevent wrinkling while rolling. While you're painting you may as well paint a design on it, and this takes us into the fascinating realm of professional scene painting. An introduction to some of its basic principles is now called for. We assume you're not too familiar with the intricacies of this splendid form of art—and that gives us courage to expound a few ideas.

Painting curtains and scenes

Don't bother with expensive theatrical canvas. Unbleached muslin is the best material you can use to make scenery and roll curtains. It is cheap, durable, and very workable. From your paint store you will need ground glue, whiting, and a fairly wide variety of powdered colors. (Buy it in half-pound lots; it's a lot more economical.)

When you have measured out the length and width of the muslin you need, nail it loosely on a frame. After you have given it a preliminary coat, it will be stretched tightly. This first coat is called "size." To make it, take a cupful of your ground glue and add it to a quart of hot water. Stir over a low flame until the glue has completely dissolved. Then mix about a cupful of this solution with two quarts of cold water and you have your sizing. Now mix a cupful of whiting with enough water to make it into a thick cream solution. Add about a third of this solution to your sizing and paint the entire surface of the muslin. Using whiting in addition to the glue sizing will give you a nice smooth surface for your colors. Two quarts should cover about twenty-five square feet of material. It takes about two hours for size to dry.

When the size is completely dry, sketch or trace in your design with charcoal. Mix your powdered colors with cold water to form a thick cream consistency. Then size solution is added in sufficient quantity so that the color mixture is neither too thick to paint with nor so thin that it will run. It is a very smart idea to try out each color on a piece of stray muslin before you start painting your scenery to be sure that it is well mixed. If the color rubs off when it is dry it means that you didn't add enough glue to your sizing.

Paint in one color after the other, always making sure wherever colors are to touch each other that the one is completely dry before you paint in the next. It may be necessary to outline some of the colors to bring out the drawing of your set: black or a very much darker shade of the same color will do the trick. Shadows can be also put in with black or with a darker shade of the color itself.

Above all keep your settings simple; paint nothing more in them than is absolutely essential to the play. If you get too fancy, and fill in your set with too many distracting details, you'll find the audience paying more attention to it than to your marionettes' emoting. For the same reason plan the colors used in your settings carefully so that they have an harmonious relationship to the colors of the costumes. At the same time don't be afraid to use bold and definite colors

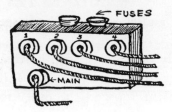

Switchboard

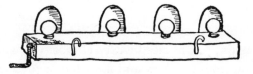

Footlights

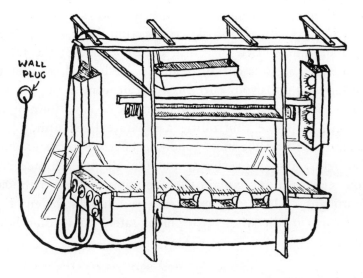

Lights in place

LIGHTING EQUIPMENT

99

for your set; the back row of your audience might like to see the set, too.

When your setting is completely painted, remove it from the frame and trim the edges. Get two round sticks the full length of the scene. Tack one to the top and the other to the bottom edge. This will enable you to roll the setting neatly and will also hold it stretched in place when in use on the stage.

Lighting

Again, you're faced with a choice: you can use the makeshift arrangement of desk and floor lamps (described in the puppet theatre section) or you can have a first-rate professional lighting system. Unless you're pretty much of an expert electrician, don't try to rig it up yourself. Take your problem to a licensed electrician and have him work out for you a switchboard with a one-socket connection that can be plugged into any wall outlet. Placed at the same side of the theatre framework as your curtain controls are located, so that the person who pulls your curtains also can work the lights, they are an ideal set-up. The switchboard can have four or five outlets, each one controlling a separate light unit, placed where it will do the most good. An effective arrangement is footlights, a strip overhead, and one down each side. Ask your electrician to explain the operation of the switchboard thoroughly. Above all, make sure you have sufficient light and can run the whole equipment safely on regular house current.

Finishing touches

The only thing left to complete your marionette theatre is the covering over the front proscenium. You can use sateen, silk, velvet, burlap, or even oilcloth. It is a simple matter to measure off your lengths and nail them in place. But if you are very ambitious, you might try covering each of the frames with unbleached muslin; size them exactly the same way as you did your scenery, sketch in an appropriate design, and paint with scene paint a decorative theatre front, as gay as only a marionette theatre can be, and yet not so arresting

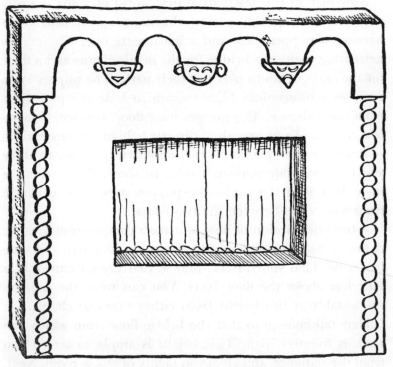

A PAINTED THEATRE FRONT

that it will hold the attention of your audience after the curtain is up.

Now, we have something really interesting for you: you know how to make puppets and their theatre, and marionettes and theirs—why not combine them into one show? The settings and stage equipment may be used for both, and think of the fun you can have staging a performance using all of your creations. You can also bring in more of your pupils or friends to help you run the show. You can have the great pleasure of teaching them how to manipulate your figures. It makes for fine spirit. And who hasn't secretly wanted to make a marionette jump and bow to his command?

Now that all this fascinating new world of yours is ready to begin, let's quickly review the not-too-great differences between a puppet stage and a marionette one. The marionette stage requires a bridge for the manipulators and a floor for the marionettes to play out their parts. The puppet stage requires a proscenium high enough to hide the puppeteer from the audience. The puppet stage floor, you will remember, consists of a narrow shelf directly behind the proscenium —and make sure there is enough unobstructed space to allow you to move your puppets freely. In short, the marionette stage floor is at the back—the puppet stage floor is at the front with a gap between the two floors.

A brief description of how to make a combination theatre: A fine, workable size would be about ten feet high and nine feet wide. Plan your proscenium so that the bottom of it is four feet above the floor level. You can work the puppets comfortably at this height from either stools or chairs. Get ladders tall enough so that the bridge floor from which you work is five feet high. This height is ample to screen you from the audience, and gives you plenty of elbow room. Next, make the stage floor, for the marionettes, eighteen inches wide and the stage floor for the puppets eight inches wide. Allow for a one-foot space between the two stage floors. This makes the distance from your front proscenium to your back bridge a little over three feet (see illustration). The bracings for the theatre, the scenery, the curtain, the lighting equipment—all follow the general principles already outlined.

A COMBINATION PUPPET AND
MARIONETTE THEATRE

After your equipment is built and your marionettes made, there are still many things to consider before you can produce a smooth and interesting show. Don't be alarmed—it's nothing drastic and doesn't require your building anything more or hiring an impresario: just a few simple rules for greater efficiency—the little things that mean the difference between an amateur and a professional show.

During a performance you must know exactly where everything is. Puppets, scenery, properties, music, and other stage effects must be within easy reaching distance and each in its proper place. Before you pull your curtain, take a quick look around and make sure you have everything you need and that you can get what you want without looking in several places; if need be, you should be able to reach behind you and pick what you want without looking. So arrange your props systematically and with a sense of order. Scene changes ought to be made quickly and noiselessly. In planning and constructing your equipment, always remember to allow sufficient space and to make everything flexible enough for a quick patch job—if the emergency arises.

Keep your productions simple. Omit anything that might prove an obstruction. No matter how fond you are of a very special idea or gadget, if it's in the way during rehearsal, scrap it. Never plan scenery that takes a long time to set up or "strike," which means clearing your stage. Remember always that scenery, properties, and costumes must never interfere with your performers, who are the main attraction. A final warning—and about time—before you cross the magic threshold into the tiny land of make-believe: In stringing your marionettes, manfully resist attaching strings that might easily become a tangled network. Use as few strings as possible.

ON WITH THE PLAY!

—<☼>—

Now that the hardest part of the job is done, you can't just sit back on your laurels and admire your handiwork. To start you off a few plays are included that you are welcome to use or to adapt. There is the rather ambitious "Pinocchio;" you'll need many puppets and props, but you can manage it. Then there is "Jack and the Beanstalk," and the ever-popular "Cinderella." Finally there is "Mr. Rabbit's Easter Jamboree," a brief, easy-to-put-on sketch which can be used for a curtain raiser. Or you may prefer writing your own plays.

There are a few basic rules to follow in putting on both original plays and those selected from other sources. Do not clutter the stage with all kinds of scenery or properties. It is quite as important to leave out things as it is to show them. Color is very important, and the right use of it, in addition to imagination and a few essential bits of scenery to suggest the place of action, will produce amazing results.

Keep your dialogue simple and to the point. Individual characters should be dressed in distinctive costumes that suggest their personalities and their voices should carry out this idea. Avoid long speeches, particularly to the audience. The characters should explain themselves and the plot by action, dialogue, and costume.

Don't be afraid of using marionettes and puppets in the same play. They can add immeasurably to the versatility of your show. We've described a simple stage that will accommodate all these types. If you are using animals, invent definite sounds for them which will leave no doubt in the audience's mind as to exactly what sort of beast they are.

Time a full three-act show so that it doesn't run over an hour and a half; beyond that it's hard to keep an audience interested. It's also tiring for the manipulators to work that long a period. Keep your intermissions short—about ten minutes is long enough. Over that there is always the danger of losing the thread of the story. Run up your curtain, ready to begin the play, at exactly the time you announced it.

All this, of course, requires rehearsal; plenty of rehearsal. Keep rehearsing your manipulators and marionettes until you are all letter perfect. A missed cue or bad timing will ruin your show.

Make sure that whoever is appointed to take care of the curtain is given the right cues for lowering and raising at exactly the right moment. This timing is very important. Keep rehearsing until there is no possibility of a slip-up.

Music is a great help to a performance and during the intermission. The best and the most inexpensive kind is recorded music. Choose pieces that suit the mood and characters of your play. A few minutes before curtain time serenade your audience with an overture of lively music. Give them a chance to settle down. Much depends on how you start. The puppeteers should be in their places, all set with their marionettes, ready to go into action smoothly after the curtain rises. When the overture is over, put on another suitable record, let it play for a few seconds, then raise your curtain slowly and let the music fade out. If your start is right it's almost certain to carry through smoothly to the end.

Always be prepared to meet emergencies. Your lights may suddenly blow out; a marionette's head strings may get hopelessly tangled; the scenery may collapse. You must be practical and quick to act in these nerve-wracking moments and do nothing that will spoil the show. If, by chance, something does go wrong, drop the curtain quickly and trot out a puppet that hasn't appeared in the play (dress him as you like) and have him announce to the audience that he is the infallible Mr. Fixit, and this accident is just what he expected because no one ever takes his advice and isn't it lucky he just happened to be passing. Give him a joke or two to tell or a song to sing or dance to. As he is amusing the audience, quickly repair your gear. You can insert a little business here by having Mr. Fixit shout backstage as to how you're getting along and don't you want any intelligent help. A voice can shout back something insulting and Mr. Fixit goes back into his routine. But the moment you've repaired the damage, yank Mr. Fixit off the stage and go ahead as if nothing had happened. This is only one suggestion; you can work out something along these lines and probably come up with all sorts of usable ideas for meeting emergencies—but try not to have them.

One idea for starting your show is just before curtain time suddenly pop a marionette's head through the curtain and ask for everybody's strict attention:

"Ladies and gents and boys and girls," he shouts. "Today we have the great pleasure in presenting a play that has delighted the crowned heads of Europe and Brooklyn. The name of this play is . . . well, it's about—it's a very fine play and the author worked awfully hard in writing this play. He calls it . . . people say it's the best thing he ever wrote . . . (in desperation) . . . it's really a very good play and . . . everybody knows it . . ." (he loudly whispers): "don't go away folks. I'll be right back. Got to see that everything is all right back here. You just can't trust these people any more."

His voice is heard backstage bellowing: "What is the name of this play? Somebody must know its name. It's only a short name." Nobody tells him. He pops his head through the cur-

tain again and dolefully says: "I think the name of this play
is . . ." He is now obviously struck with an idea. A light
can be suddenly flashed over his head. "Boys and girls, do
you know the name of this here play. Bet you don't."

You may be certain that the boys and girls will delightedly
shout back the name of the play. At this, the puppet wags
his head impudently and quickly says as he disappears:

"Ha! I knew it all the time. Just wanted to see if you did."

And now you're off and on your own. It's been a lot of
work making these marionettes and the stage for them to
act on and the choosing of the plays for them, but it's also
been a lot of fun and you'll find the thrills of being a marionette impresario (or that is what you will be) are richly
rewarding. On with the play!

MR. RABBIT'S EASTER JAMBOREE

A PLAY IN ONE SCENE

❋

Characters

MR. RABBIT

THE FROG

THE TIGER

MR. RABBIT'S EASTER JAMBOREE

A play in one act and one scene; in which MR. RABBIT, *the* FROG, *and the* TIGER, *are the only characters. Some others are talked about but never appear, which considerably reduces the problem of constructing them.*

In producing this play it will be necessary to work out several technical details which will make it possible for things to happen as they should. For instance, an audience is always delighted to see a puppet drop something he is carrying and pick it up again. Mr. Rabbit in this play should set his basket down at least once. To make him drop his basket, the following preparations are necessary:

1. Take a string about a foot longer than the distance between Mr. Rabbit's paw and the control and tie it to the handle of the basket.
2. Pass the string through a hole in Mr. Rabbit's paw so that it slides easily.
3. Fasten the loose end of the string to the control.

To pick up the basket, pull the string—to set it down, release the string. If the string is long enough it will be possible for Mr. Rabbit to walk a few steps away from the basket without moving it.

One of the eggs in the basket should be separate from the others and attached to a string. This will solve the business of giving it to the Frog so that he can throw it out of the pond when Mr. Rabbit gives him the signal. Some comic business can be created by dangling the egg in front of the Tiger to tantalize him, before it settles itself in the basket with the other eggs.

The pond is one of the essential bits of scenery and should be practicable. All that is needed is a hole in the stage floor, large enough for the Frog to appear and disappear. This is technically called a "trap," which can be shut for other scenes. The bare edges of the trap can be hidden by a strip of water weeds and flowers, not too high, painted on cardboard, and placed in front or, to be technical again, on the downstage side of the trap. A backdrop with trees and flowers to represent the woods will be required to make the scene complete. At the end of the play Tiger the Terror yanks so hard to pull his tail loose that he leaves it behind. Therefore make the tail separately and tack it very lightly in place so that when pulled with a little force it will come loose.

A word about characterization. The repetitions of the Frog should be stressed and they could even be increased with good effect. They should sound like the bass croakings of a frog, and have a definite rhythm. Mr. Rabbit's lines might be best spoken in a high-pitched, shrill voice. When he talks to the Tiger about the magic pond, he should change to a mysterious, monotonous tone, spoken more slowly. Obviously the Tiger speaks in a gruff voice and is very much the bully. For occasional growling, especially at the end when he becomes furious, the use of a kazoo is very effective. If these suggestions are followed, contrast, color, and comedy will result.

THE SCENE—IN A THICK PART OF THE FOREST

In the center of the stage is a fair-sized pond bordered by weeds, cattails, and water lilies.

When the curtain rises, the Frog *is seen splashing in and out just for practice.*

MR. RABBIT *enters singing a gay song and carrying a basket of Easter eggs.*

FROG *(coming out of pond)*: Ba gump, ba gump! Well, well, you sound happy this morning, Mr. Rabbit.

MR. RABBIT: Good morning, old man Frog. Hello! Happy? Yes, sir! Got a basketful of good news. Yes, sir!

FROG: Whatcha got, whatcha got, whatcha got?

MR. RABBIT: Take a look, old man Frog. Eggs! Brand-new Easter eggs . . . all colors. Yes, sir!

FROG: Yes, sir! Yes, sir!

BOTH: Yes, sir! Yes, sir! Yes, sir!

FROG: Whereju get 'em? Whereju get 'em? Whereju get 'em?

MR. RABBIT: From my friends in the barnyard yonder. We're having a grand Easter jamboree in my hutch on the hill. Going over to decorate the place now. The hens and their little chicks are all coming over. Yes, sir!

FROG: Sounds grand, sounds grand. Sounds like a grand party. Yes, sir! Guess you're not inviting any more guests.

MR. RABBIT: Well, there'll be room for one or two more. 'Fact, I was just going to throw some pebbles in the water to see if you were in.

FROG: Guess I am, guess I am—and I haven't made any dates yet. No, sir! No, sir! No, sir!

MR. RABBIT: Well then, come over to the jamboree, old man Frog, about seven o'clock and bring your wife along.

FROG: You bet, you bet, you bet! Seven o'clock. Shall I bring my banjo?

MR. RABBIT: Oh, yeah. I was going to ask you—bring your banjo. We'll be in a festive mood. If you want to come early you can help me put the eggs around so they look pretty-like.

FROG: You bet, you bet, you bet!

MR. RABBIT: So long, 'till later.

TIGER (*singing offstage*): I'm looking for something. I'm looking for something. I'm looking for something and I'm not blind. I'm looking for something. I'm looking for something. I'm looking for something that I can't find.

MR. RABBIT: Jerusalem! That sounds like Tiger the Terror!

FROG: It sure does! It sure does! It sure is! It sure is!

MR. RABBIT: Crippling crickets, let me hide!

FROG: Jump in, jump in, jump in!

MR. RABBIT: Oh, dear, no! Not in there. I'm a rabbit, not a frog!

FROG: I forgot, I forgot, I forgot! Let me hide the eggs in the pond.

MR. RABBIT: Yes . . . No! What'll I do? He'll see me if I run . . . And I wouldn't get very far . . . And he'll smell the eggs—Guess he smells them already.

FROG: Oh, dear! Oh, dear! Too bad! Too bad!

MR. RABBIT: I know what! Got to use my wits! Only way out! Take a chance! He's not too smart. Listen, old man Frog.

FROG: What, what, what?

MR. RABBIT: I'm going to sit with my tail in the water. Put the basket here. If Tiger asks you what you're doin' I'll say, "Buzz, buzz, buzz." (*Whispers to* FROG.) You take this egg down with you. When I say "Up they come," you throw the egg out of the water and I'll catch it in the basket. Take this thick rope too. When I say "Don't move" you —buzz, buzz, buzz. (*Whispers again.*) You get the idea?

FROG: I getcha, I getcha, I getcha!

MR. RABBIT: If it doesn't work, there won't be any jamboree tonight. (TIGER *is heard singing again.*) Here he comes. Duck!

FROG: Okay, okay, okay!

MR. RABBIT: Oh, Easter-egg Angel, bring me luck!

TIGER (*entering*): I'm looking for something. I'm looking for

something all the day. I'm looking for something. I'm look-
ing for something. I'm looking for a needle in the hay.
Well, look what I found! Charmed to see you, Mr. Rabbit!
And look what you got!

MR. RABBIT: Sh! Mr. Tiger the Terror! I'm surprised at you!
Don't disturb the magic!

TIGER: MAGIC! What magic?

MR. RABBIT: Don't you know this is Easter-egg zone? Look!
Look at the eggs. But don't make any noise.

TIGER: I see the eggs. They look fine—delicious.

MR. RABBIT: There's more coming.

TIGER: Coming from where?

MR. RABBIT: From where? The pond, of course.

TIGER: What are you sitting in the pond for?

MR. RABBIT: Sh! To conjure up the Easter eggs—all colors!

TIGER: Ridiculous! Don't you look funny—ha, ha, ha, ha!
I might as well have a good laugh before I eat you for
breakfast. Good for the appetite—ha, ha, ha, ha!

MR. RABBIT: Not so funny if you can conjure up hundreds
of eggs—thousands. You have to come and spoil it.

TIGER: Say, what's the idea?

MR. RABBIT: Like this. Every Easter eve from sunrise to
sunset this pond conjures up big fresh Easter eggs—all
colors. But you must put your tail in the pond, and sit
quiet and concentrate. Wish I had a longer tail. A tail like
yours ought to conjure them by dozens.

TIGER: You don't mean it!

MR. RABBIT: Mean it! Wait and see! But you must be quiet!
My ancestors have been conjuring for generations. You sit
quiet—like this . . . and pretty soon—up they come! Up
they come! Up they come! (*An egg comes flying out of the
water.*)

TIGER: Boy, oh boy! An egg! Well, I'll be—

MR. RABBIT: Come on, sit, Mr. Tiger Terror!

TIGER: You're not fooling me.

MR. RABBIT: You saw, didn't you?

TIGER: That's right. I saw—

MR. RABBIT: Hush up and you'll see plenty more.

TIGER: Put your tail in the pond, like this. *(He sits next to* MR. RABBIT.)

MR. RABBIT: That's right. Get in it—way down in.

TIGER: It's wet!

MR. RABBIT: Hush now! And whatever you feel, don't move!

TIGER: Something's tickling the end of my tail.

MR. RABBIT: Don't move! That's the conjure spirits trying the magic. Don't move—don't move!

TIGER: Don't have to holler—I'm not deaf—I can hear you.

MR. RABBIT: I want to make sure, 'cause if you move the magic won't tie.

TIGER: Feels like the magic was tying on pretty tight.

MR. RABBIT: It does? You sure? Good sign.

TIGER: Getting tighter and tighter. Feels like I'm anchored. Couldn't move if I wanted to.

MR. RABBIT: All the better.

TIGER: When do the eggs come up?

MR. RABBIT: Sh! You got to concentrate now. Don't talk no more until the magic winds up. Okay?

FROG *(popping out of pond)*: Okay, okay, okay!

TIGER: What's that?

MR. RABBIT: Sh! Echo of the conjure spirits—they're working. Sit still now. I'm going to empty the basket and bring it back so you can catch the eggs in it.

TIGER: Hurry up!

MR. RABBIT: You sit there. The longer you sit, the bigger the eggs. Old man Frog, did you tie it good and tight?

FROG: Good and tight! Good and tight! Good and tight!

MR. RABBIT *(picking up his basket of eggs)*: I'll be back by-and-by. And if I don't come back before next week, jump in the pond, because that tail of yours, Mr. Tiger the Terrible, is not coming out no more!

TIGER: Wait a minute! Come back here! Come back! I'll tear you to pieces if you leave me here. Come back! *(Growls, pulls, yanks until he yanks his tail off. He runs off yelping. MR. RABBIT and the FROG and the tiger's tail dance together in glee. Then pull your curtain. If the audience applauds, draw your curtain again for bows.)*

JACK AND THE BEANSTALK

A PLAY IN THREE SCENES

—<✧>—

Characters

JACK
HIS MOTHER
THE COW
THE FARMER
THE OGRESS
THE GIANT

JACK AND THE BEANSTALK

Costumes:

THE OGRESS: She wears a dress made of a coarse brown burlap with green buttons. Her wig may be of frayed rope.

THE GIANT: The giant should wear a false beard made of buckram or cardboard, with black rope for hair and whiskers. His huge cloak is made of green duvetyn. His boots are black oilcloth with wooden soles.

JACK'S MOTHER: She wears a dress of dark blue wash material with a gay colored shawl. Her clothes should look badly worn.

JACK: Jack may wear any ordinary pair of trousers and an old shirt, both very much worn and patched. His cap should also be old.

THE COW: The head of the cow may be made of buckram or cardboard covered with white duvetyn of which the rest of the costume may be made. Black spots may be painted on it.

Properties:

Bag of beans.

The beanstalks are made of rope, with leaves and bean pods of green cloth.

Jack's house. It is made of an ordinary screen with paper tacked on it. The roof is red and the walls brown.

A milestone made of cardboard.

Trees made of cardboard tacked on sticks of wood.

The hen and the golden egg. The hen may be made of cardboard and painted red, black, and white. A darning egg painted gold will serve as the hen's golden egg.

The three bags filled with gold which Jack throws down.

A caldron in which the ogress cooks the giant's food. An iron pot may be used or a large fruit basket covered with black tissue paper.

The ax Jack uses to chop the beanstalks. It is made of wood painted silver with a black handle.

In this play the action of one scene can be lapped into the action of the following scene, for in this way the dropping of the curtain too often is eliminated. The method will be described as the play progresses.

SCENE ONE. *Outside* JACK'S *house. There is a little cottage where* JACK *and his* MOTHER *live. This may or may not have a practicable door. A simple screen with paper tacked on and painted will be sufficient to give the effect. A little farther back than the house there should be a low hedge behind which the beanstalks can be hidden on the floor. The beanstalks are attached to strings which pass through screw eyes in the ceiling. At the proper moment someone hidden from view may pull the beanstalks into place by means of these strings. When the curtain rises* JACK *and his* MOTHER *are on the scene. She may be seated at the doorstep or on a stool with* JACK *at her feet.*

MOTHER: I don't know what I shall give you to eat today, my son. We ate up the last half loaf of bread last night, and the cow won't give a drop of milk.

JACK: Don't trouble yourself about me, good mother. It is I, big and sturdy as I am, who should be looking after you. But this day I shall surely go out into the world and make my fortune.

MOTHER: Alas, my son, it isn't your fault if Heaven hasn't given you the wits that other men have. We must get along the best we can.

JACK: Now, mother, I'm telling you that I intend to go out into the world and make my fortune.

MOTHER: I should like to help you—but I haven't so much as a pair of new breeches to hide your legs with. But I have an idea. I have decided to part with the cow because she gives no milk. Tie a rope about her neck and lead her to the fair and see how much you can sell her for.

JACK: Willingly, mother. I will fetch her this minute and I warrant I'll show you that I can drive as good a bargain as any. (JACK *goes off to get the* Cow.)

MOTHER: Heaven aid his simple wits and make them bring more than the cow is worth.

(JACK *returns with the* Cow *which is heard mooing as they enter.*)

JACK: So, mother, bid me farewell, for your son will soon become a man of the world.

MOTHER: Fare you well, my son. Mind you take heed of the snares and traps you will surely find along the way.

JACK: And so I will, mother, I'll remember it well, and keep an eye open this side and that. Good-by, little mother.

MOTHER: Good luck. (*Kissing* JACK *good-by on the top of the head, she enters the house.*)

JACK: Come, my lady. I intend to take thee to a very gay and merry fair and thou must walk nimbly, for I am in high spirits this day. It is the first day of my manhood. Dost understand and art of the same mind?

COW: Moo!

JACK: Faith, thou has more brains beneath thy horn than men give thee credit for. And if I fail to see some of the snares and traps and whatnots, that thy mistress, my mother, spoke of, do not fail to tell me of it, dost hear?

COW: Moo!

JACK: And since we are agreed, let us proceed to this fair.

(JACK *and the* COW *start on their way to the fair. They go through the movements of walking without actually going from the same spot. The cottage is slid off the scene behind them. From the other side of the stage, a tree moves in their direction and passes across the stage and off. The tree can be made of cardboard tacked on a stick and can be carried across the stage by a person concealed behind it. Two milestones pass* JACK *and the* COW *across the stage in the same manner. While these objects are passing him,* JACK *sings his song as he presumably walks along.)*

JACK: Heigh ho, away we go.

> The sun swings high and the sun hangs low,
> But heigh ho, away we go,
> Me and my lady, oh.
> She walketh high and she walketh so
> While the sun he sinketh very low
> Heigh ho, away we go.

(The third milestone stops in front of JACK *and the* COW.)

JACK: Now there, my lady. Let us see how far we have come. *(Looks at milestone.)* Three miles. Faith, I think we have earned a rest. What does my lady think?

COW: Moo!

JACK: We do get along well together. 'Tis a pity we should be separated. Had I known sooner that thou wast such a companion I would have taken thee for many a walk. But knowledge until this day hath always been kept away from me, for thou must know that I am a very simple fellow and now I am a man of the world by three miles. Didst see any traps and snares and things along the way?

COW: Moo, moo.

JACK: I did not either. Let us get along now for I am impatient to walk into some more knowledge of this world.

(They continue and one more milestone passes them by.

JACK *sings again and they meet a* FARMER.)

FARMER: Hail and good day to you, my lad. You seem happy enough.

JACK: Good day to you, countryman. And why shouldn't I be happy? Isn't this the first day when I shall become a man of the world and make my fortune?

FARMER: And whither do you go?

JACK: I am going to the fair with my lady cow, and there I shall drive a very smart bargain.

FARMER: Do you mean to sell the cow?

JACK: If that is the way to drive a bargain, that is what I mean to do.

FARMER: 'Tis a good cow—gentle enough and not too tough. This is a fine cow. But she is no finer than these precious things I have in my sack.

JACK: And what may those precious things be?

FARMER: Take a look for yourself.

JACK: I think I should have seen something like them before but I do admit that I never did behold a parcel of beans that were as precious as these. In them I am sure I perceive the knowledge and the riches of the world. What are they?

FARMER: You may think they are beans, but they are not. They are very precious jewels. 'Tis not a bad cow.

JACK: Let us make a bargain here and now. If you will give me your bag of beans I will give you my cow.

FARMER: I will gladly make this bargain with you, lad, to encourage you on your way in the world. I assure you I make it at a loss to myself.

JACK: Wait a moment. (*To* Cow): Tell me, my lady, if I am contriving a good bargain?

Cow: Moo.

JACK: Here is the cow, good countryman.

FARMER: And here is the sack, lad, and take care you do not lose it.

JACK: I will take good care, sir, and I will watch this side and that side for traps and snares as my mother bade me. And I thank you for this excellent bargain. Good day to you.

(JACK goes off the stage. The FARMER goes off with the COW in the opposite direction. The action of the passing landscape is reversed. JACK who is on his way back home can be heard singing off stage. His voice gets louder and louder until he reappears on the scene one mile from the cottage.)

JACK: Heigh ho! the sun swings low,
　　The sun swings very, very low,
　　For me and my lady, oh.
　　Heigh ho! the sun hangs high
　　The sun hangs very, very high,
　　For 'tis by, my lady, good-by,
　　And the sun swings low and the sun hangs high,
　　So, my lady, so good-by, good-by.

(He sits on the milestone.)

Jack, my man, thou art now a full-hatched man of the world, truly thou art. Surely this fine bargain will make thy mother very happy and proud. Never again will the neighbors call thee simpleton. I do hope my lady cow will be happy with her new master. She maketh a good companion, it is true. But she is no use beyond that; I do wonder that the countryman did make the bargain with me. Thou art a smart lad, Jack, that thou art.

(JACK continues on his way home. The milestone goes off, the tree passes him, and the cottage is brought back in its place.)

For heigho, away we go,
Away, away, away we go. *(Repeat whole song.)*

And here we are at home, my bargain and me. Mother, mother, I have come back.

MOTHER *(comes out of the house)*: What my son, are you back already? But what did you do with the cow? You've hardly been gone long enough to reach the fair, and you are back.

JACK: Ah, mother dear, most men have to go to the fair to make their fortunes, but your son has done better. I found a fortune all ready waiting for me on the way.

MOTHER: And what fortune is that, simple son?

JACK: Look in there and you will see for yourself.

MOTHER *(takes sack of beans)*: A fortune, indeed. You've got here a sack of common beans. And what have you done with the cow?

JACK: I exchanged her for this sack of precious pearls, mother. There was a countryman hailed me good day and I him —"Whither goest thou?" he asked. "To the fair," quoth I, "to sell this cow." " 'Tis a good cow," quoth he, "but not as good as this sack of precious stones." "Let us make a bargain," quoth I, "for your sack I will give thee my cow." And in a twinkling we made a bargain.

MOTHER: So you gave the cow for this handful of dirty beans.

JACK: But they are not beans, mother. They may look to you like beans—they are precious stones. He told me so himself and I know it.

MOTHER: Well, this much for thy precious stones, thou simpleton. Mayhap now they'll grow thee a fortune.

(She snatches the sack of beans from JACK *and flings them somewhere at the back of the scene.)* My son, there is only one method of teaching thee. *(She rushes into the house.)*

JACK: But, mother, you are throwing away the first fortune I ever made. Wisdom do be a queer thing.

MOTHER *(returning with a broom)*: And when you make another bargain, son of mine, think first as many times as I lay this broom on thy back. *(She beats* JACK *soundly with the broom and then goes into the house.)*

JACK: 'Tis a very queer world, I'm thinking. For the sake of a cow that was a very good companion, I am robbed of a fortune and get me a good beating on my back. I hope the countryman had better luck. As for thee, Jack, what wilt thou do next? Thou art tired in the legs and in the back. Go into the house and rest, for tomorrow thou must go out into the world again.

(Goes into house.)

(The scene darkens by degrees. A huge beanstalk grows slowly out of the ground next to the house. It grows taller and taller as the scene gets darker and darker and then lighter and lighter. The top of the beanstalk grows high out of sight. The crowing of a cock is heard, and JACK *comes out of the house.)*

JACK: It is a bright morning that greets me and my empty stomach. Thy foot will be all the lighter, Jack, my man, for thou must walk today surely until thou meet'st Fortune. Well, well, what is this? I do not remember this. It grows so high I cannot see the top. Of course, Jack thou simpleton, this is the beanstalk that grew out of the precious beans thy mother threw on the ground. I have a great curiosity to see the top. In that case thou must climb, Jack, so the sooner thou startest the later thou'lt think about it.

*(*JACK *goes behind the house where the stalks grow thickest, climbs on a concealed table and then on a stool on top of the table. Just a hand, a foot, or his head appears now and then through the stalks.)*

JACK: Heigh ho, away we go,
 As high as the sun swings low.
 Heigh ho—higher ho,
 High and high and higher ho,
 High as the sun swings low.
 (His voice grows fainter as he seems to reach the top.
JACK'S MOTHER *comes out of the house and looks around for the lad.)*
MOTHER: Jack! Ho, Jack! I hear him, but I don't see him anywhere. Ho, Jack! The good saints preserve us, what's this? Bless me, if it isn't a huge beanstalk and it's the exact place where I threw the beans last night. Jack! Ho, Jack! (JACK *is heard singing faintly.)* He's gone and climbed it. Jack! Ho! Come down or you'll break your neck. Heaven preserve him! Heaven preserve him! He's got it into his head to seek his fortune and fifty thousand devils won't hinder him. It is a burden truly to be blessed with poverty and a simple son. *(She sits down by her door and weeps in her apron.* JACK'S *voice can still be heard very faintly as the curtain falls.)*

SCENE TWO *is the land of the* GIANT *which is at the top of the beanstalk. There is a huge table covered with a cloth in the center of the stage. Two or three stray beanstalks hang in back of the table. There is a cauldron to one side, the contents of which the* OGRESS *is busily stirring with a large spoon as the curtain rises.*
OGRESS: Boil over pot,
 Get good and hot,
 Or the giant will like it not.
 *(*JACK *is heard singing his song.)*
I hear a queer noise, a very queer noise. That's not the Giant's voice.

(J ACK *appears among the beanstalks.*)

JACK: And this is the place where the sun swings high and the sun hangs low. I like this country. Good morning, grandmother. How do you do today?

OGRESS: Good evening to you, my lad, for it is evening and not morning.

JACK: Oh, that makes little difference, grandmother, for I like a good evening as well. Let me help you, grandmother. I think my arm is stronger to stir the pot.

OGRESS: Thank thee, lad. (J ACK *stirs ambitiously.*) Dost know where thou art?

JACK: Not yet. But I will find out, and if Fortune doth live here, I would meet her.

OGRESS: There isn't a doubt thou wilt find out. Know, my lad, that this is the abode of an evil giant who for the most part does eat children and young lads for his dinner. I'm sure thou wouldst not be distasteful to him.

JACK: Ah, but he will not eat me, grandmother. No giant has ever eaten me.

OGRESS: Alas, young lad, he will surely eat thee if he finds thee here. He will be here in a very short time now, so be prudent and climb down where you came from as quickly as possible. I could not see a good lad like thee make a roast for this giant.

JACK: I have a great curiosity to see this giant, grandmother, and you need not fear that he will eat me. You will be as good as to hide me somewhere. I have heard wonderful tales about giants.

OGRESS: There are wonderful things here, to be sure, and if thou art as brave as thou sayest, I will hide thee that thou mayst see what wonderful things there are. I fear that he might smell thee, however. In that case I will manage somehow. After supper he plays with his magic toys and then does always fall asleep. It is when he is asleep that you must make your escape.

JACK: I will do that, grandmother, and I will repay you however I can.

(Steps of the GIANT *are heard.)*

OGRESS: I hear the giant's footsteps. He will be here in a moment. Hide quickly under the table.

(JACK *hides and the* GIANT *enters.)*

GIANT: Ahee, ahi, ahoo, ahum,
   I smell young living flesh, by gum.

OGRESS: 'Tis the bristles of a young pig the wind is blowing about. I scaled it not long ago.

GIANT: Aha, aha, aha, achu!

OGRESS: Good appetite. You should feel better now.

GIANT *(smells very loudly)*:
   Ahee, aho, ahi, ahum,
   By gee, by jo, by jum.

OGRESS: Sit down now and I will give you a good supper. Did you go far this day?

GIANT: Not so far—one hundred and fifty miles to the north; three hundred miles to the south and six hundred miles to the west—not so far.

OGRESS: Did you bring much?

GIANT: Not so much—ten cows, forty sheep, twenty bags of corn, four kegs of wine, and twelve children—not so much.

OGRESS: You must be tired and hungry.

(She fills a bowl from the cauldron and puts it before him.)

GIANT: Not so tired and not so hungry.

(He devours the contents with one gulp and sniffs once more.)

   Ahee, aho, ahi, ahum,
   I smell, I smell, I smell, by gum.

(The Ogress *brings the whole pot to him. He eats from the pot and then sweeps it off the table.)* Old woman, bring me my golden hen—my little golden hen. *(She brings in the little hen and sets it on the table.)* Bring me my bags of gold. My treasure, my little hackle cackle, art thou well? *(The hen cackles in response.)*

(The Ogress *brings in three bags of gold and lays them on the table and then goes out.)*

Giant: Now lay me thy golden egg. *(The hen presumably lays the golden egg each time.)* Now lay me thy golden egg. Now lay me thy golden egg. Now lay me thy golden egg. Now lay me thy golden egg.

(The Giant *nods and slowly falls to sleep; the hen stops cackling and also falls asleep;* Jack *comes from his hiding place and examines the treasures.)*

Jack: This is a most peculiar hen, and I have my mind to take it with me. Jack, my man, Fortune is here well met, so if thou take it not, it will be no fault of Fortune. The giant does sleep prodigiously. I will throw these sacks of gold down first for luck. *(*Jack *presumably drops the sacks of gold down the beanstalk one by one. The* Giant *snores.)* Come my little hackle cackle, I believe that is thy name. *(As* Jack *takes up the hen, it cackles loudly, thus awakening the* Giant. Jack *disappears down the beanstalk back of the table.)* Not so much noise, my little hackle cackle. *(But the hen cackles even more loudly.)*

Giant: Ahi, ahi, ahee, ahoo, ah chu! What is it, my little hackle cackle? *(*Giant *discovers that the gold and the hen have disappeared. He bellows, whips out his huge dagger, and begins to descend the beanstalk.)* Who carries away my little hen? Stop, thou insect, or I'll slit thee presently and boil, broil, roast and slice thee!

Ogress *(who has come in at the* Giant's *awakening)*: Poor lad, poor lad, poor lad!

SCENE THREE is the same as SCENE ONE. JACK'S MOTHER *sits in the door. The sacks of gold which* JACK *has dropped from the top of the beanstalk fall to the ground one after the other.*

MOTHER: Heavens! What manner of rain is this?

(She goes into the house. The mingled voices of JACK, *the* GIANT, *and the cackling hen are heard. The beanstalk begins to shake very violently. Then* JACK *appears with the hen and rushes into the house calling to his* MOTHER.)

JACK: Mother, mother! Quick! Give me the ax!

MOTHER: My son! What is happening?

JACK: The ax! The ax!

*(*JACK *reappears with a huge ax, followed by his* MOTHER. *He chops away at the beanstalk with all his might.)*

MOTHER: Jack, my man, thy wits are now in thy arms!

(The stalk falls with a great crash. The GIANT *is heard roaring and then all is quiet.)*

JACK: Well, mother, come and pick up the bags of gold about your feet.

MOTHER: Gold? They did have a peculiarly pleasant sound.

JACK: The little hen is gold, too, mother, and she does lay golden eggs. Now, mother, I will tell you how I met Fortune.

MOTHER: Son, what matters more than meeting Fortune is to treat her well.

JACK: That is what I hope to do, Mom.

MOTHER: But for now, Jack lad, get into the house and go to bed, for I think it is high time.

*(*JACK *and his* MOTHER *go into the house and go to bed. The mooing of the* COW *is heard off stage. Presently the* COW *herself appears and moos contentedly at the familiar scene. Then she knocks at the door and the curtain comes down.)*

CINDERELLA

OR

THE GLASS SLIPPER

A PLAY IN THREE SCENES

—✧—

Characters

DAISY ⎫
CHARLOTTE ⎬ *the two stepsisters of Cinderella*

CINDERELLA'S STEPMOTHER

CINDERELLA

THE FAIRY GODMOTHER

THE PRINCE

NERO, THE BUTLER

THE PAGE

LADIES AND COURTIERS

CINDERELLA

Costumes:

DAISY AND CHARLOTTE AT THE BALL: Daisy's costume may be a yellow sateen trimmed with green and gold. Her hat may be fashioned of buckram painted green and trimmed with little green and yellow pompons. Charlotte's gown should be almost exactly the same but in colors more befitting her temperament.

The gowns of the other lady guests at the ball may be fashioned in the same general style as the sisters'. Except in the cases of Charlotte and Daisy the colors of the costumes at the ball should be selected with great care. No costume of any of the guests should be as unique as those of the Prince and Cinderella.

DAISY AND CHARLOTTE AT HOME: Daisy's home dress should be of a dull yellow poplin. Charlotte's may be identical.

THE STEPMOTHER: Her dress may be made of any coarse material and should be a brown or a gray. The details of her costume should be in keeping with her character, which is not a pleasant one.

THE FAIRY GODMOTHER: The godmother's flowing gown should be of a rich blue sateen. If desired, gold paper stars may be pasted on it in a scattered design. The cuffs and the star halo can be made of buckram painted gold. They are trimmed with brass bells. Her necklace is made of brass bells also. Her wig may be made of tight-fitting blue felt, to which the halo may be sewed. The wand is a stick with a rubber ball at the end trimmed with bells.

CINDERELLA AT HOME: Her dress may be of any coarse drab or brown material. It may also have patches of other colors as well as torn places. Her shoes should be very much worn if she wears any at all.

CINDERELLA AT THE BALL: Cinderella's ball gown should be a very delicate and tasteful one. The bodice and overskirt is of Nile green silk. The skirt should be of a salmon shade of silk. The trimming should be of gold lace. The coronet can be made of buckram or gold paper. The crystal slippers may be obtained by painting a pair of slippers with aluminum paint and covering them with sheet gelatine.

NERO, THE BUTLER: His costume is of blue duvetyn with clear glass buttons and gold braid for trimming. His hat is made of felt or buckram, also blue.

The costumes of the other members of the Prince's retinue may be modeled after the butler's, with slight variations in trimming and color. One person may be both drummer and butler, or the parts may be played by two characters.

THE PRINCE: The entire costume of the Prince is of a snow-white duvetyn with trimmings of gold and red. The coat and vest should be lined with red sateen. The cuffs are trimmed with gold lace. The low boots should be of white oilcloth with high sheen. They are trimmed with red sateen. His hat should be of white felt trimmed with white plumes.

The same type of costume should be worn by the gentlemen guests at the ball in a lesser degree of elegance.

Properties:

The fireplace, which can be made of beaverboard. The arched space where the fire is should open in the middle so that the godmother can step through it and make her entrance that way. The effect of the embers is obtained by putting an electric bulb behind red tissue paper.

An ordinary kitchen table and chair. The table should be covered with a very large tablecloth that reaches to the floor.

A glass bowl filled with fruit.

A statuette, several of which may be cut out of beaverboard, painted in gay festive colors and placed around in the ballroom scene. Stars of silver and gold paper may be pasted to the background of the setting.

A toy brass trumpet for the page.

A yellow silk cushion holding the crystal slipper.

The drummer's drum.

Note: In this play magic is reduced to its simplest and most naive elements. One thing changes into another just at the mere "say-so" of the fairy creature.

SCENE ONE. *A room with a large hearth, the favorite corner of* CINDERELLA. *The furnishings are a table covered with a large tablecloth that reaches to the floor and two or three stools. There is a door to one side of the stage and a bell cord which rings when a bell is pulled. In one corner there is a closet.*

Before the curtain rises a drum and trumpet are heard in the distance. The curtain goes up, and DAISY *and* CHARLOTTE *are clapping their hands, eager to know what the festive noise is about.*

DAISY: Sh!

CHARLOTTE: A trumpet.

DAISY: A drum.

VOICE OF PAGE *(accompanied with much beating of drum and blowing of trumpet)*:
> Eye to the King's presence,
> Ear to the King's words.

DAISY: It's the King's crier again.

CHARLOTTE: Perhaps it's another grand ball.

VOICE OF PAGE *(Every sentence of his speech should be punctuated with the booming of the drum.)*: Faithful, loyal and happy subjects of the King! Young and old, gallant youths and pretty maids, give your ear to the mandate of the King!

Grand and galla, splendid and resplendent ball will take place tonight at the royal, spacious, and capacious palace of his generous Majesty, the King! All the ladies, escorted and unescorted, are invited to wear their most entrancing gowns for the eyes of the melancholy Prince to feast upon. The lamps will burn brightly all night. The musicians will never cease their music. Thousands of gay feet will dance till dawn. The Prince will dance with many ladies. Before morning he will choose a bride. You have heard the King's word! Do not fail the King!

(The sound of the trumpet and drum grows fainter and fainter as the royal procession goes off in the distance. The two sisters listen until the drums can be heard no longer, then they return to the center of the stage.)

DAISY: I will wear my new velvet gown.

CHARLOTTE: I'll wear my diamond necklace.

DAISY: The Prince is to choose a wife.

CHARLOTTE: My beauty will not escape him.

DAISY: Neither will your nose, darling. He'll see that first, then he'll smile at me.

CHARLOTTE: And, say, what comfortable feet you have. You'll never fall with those as anchors.

DAISY: The Prince will fall in love with me!

CHARLOTTE: With me!

DAISY: With me!

DAISY AND CHARLOTTE: With me! Me!

STEPMOTHER'S VOICE: Cinderella! Cinderella!

(Suddenly the stepsisters cease their quarrel at the sound of CINDERELLA'S *name.)*

CHARLOTTE: We forgot our stepsister. He may choose Cinderella.

DAISY: Of course we did forget her.

(They both laugh mockingly.)

DAISY: She has no time to see the Prince. She must watch the fire and see that the smoke goes up the chimney straight.

CHARLOTTE: And sing the ashes to sleep.

DAISY: It is the Prince who will have to visit her.

CHARLOTTE *(calling to* CINDERELLA*)*: Cinders!

DAISY: Cinderella!

CHARLOTTE: Cinders!

DAISY: Oh, Cinderella!

CHARLOTTE: Where is that Cinders?

DAISY: Now, sister, you go a tiny bit too far. You must call her Cinderella!

CHARLOTTE: Ha, ha, ha, you goose! The "ella" is unnecessary and wasteful.

DAISY: Remember we are grand ladies and should talk as such.

CHARLOTTE: Very true. Cinderella!

DAISY AND CHARLOTTE *(calling and getting more and more impatient)*: Cinderella! Cinderella! Cinderella!

STEPMOTHER'S VOICE: Stop your yelling in there! Cinderella is on the roof dusting the chimney. Didn't I tell you that yelling makes your voices coarse?

(The following speeches are shouted in answer to their MOTHER *who is off stage.)*

DAISY: It is getting late. I'll never be ready for the ball. I must have Cinderella. My shoes need polishing!

CHARLOTTE: My hair needs fixing!

DAISY: My stocking has a hole in it.

CHARLOTTE: My dress has two hooks off it.

DAISY: My hair needs fixing.

CHARLOTTE: And my ribbons tied.

DAISY AND CHARLOTTE: My petticoat needs ironing.

DAISY: The floor should be scrubbed.

CHARLOTTE: The table cleaned.

DAISY: The pots and pans.

CHARLOTTE: And the linen is dirty.

DAISY AND CHARLOTTE (*shouting more loudly than ever*): Cinderella! Cinderella! Cinderella!

STEPMOTHER (*rushing in very much annoyed and shouting with no better manners herself*): Stop yelling! Stop! Stop! I spend so much time and money to make you beautiful and the result is you croak like frogs. How can I ever find rich and elegant husbands for you if you continue with those manners? Call more sweetly, like this: "Cinderella!"

(*She calls* CINDERELLA *as sweetly as possible, but it is more like crowing than anything else, as she prolongs the last vowel.*)

DAISY AND CHARLOTTE (*imitating their mother*): Cinderella!

STEPMOTHER: That's better! Anyway, ring the bell when you want her. The bell, darlings! You must learn some time. Now don't forget it. I'll send the little fool in to wait on you. (*She goes off and a moment later she is heard calling very raucously.*) Cinderella! Cinderella! Come down here at once.

DAISY: Mother is right. We shouldn't yell. And we must not forget that it is proper to ring.

(CHARLOTTE *pulls the bell cord which rings the bell. Both sisters then take elegant poses and wait for* CINDERELLA.)

CINDERELLA (*entering and speaking in a meek gentle voice*): Do you want me, sisters?

CHARLOTTE: Yes, Cinderella. It's time to get ready for the ball. Fix my hair for me!

DAISY: Polish my shoes!

CHARLOTTE: Sew hooks on my dress!

DAISY: Darn my stockings!

CHARLOTTE: Lace me up!

DAISY: Fix my hair.

CHARLOTTE: Tie my ribbons!

DAISY: Iron my petticoat!

CHARLOTTE: Look at the dirty floor!

DAISY: Scrub it!

CHARLOTTE: Scour the pots!

DAISY: And the table!

CHARLOTTE: Wash the linen!

DAISY: And hurry and make the beds!

(The two sisters pull and jostle poor little CINDERELLA *from one end of the room to the other, making her do this and that but not allowing her to finish anything because all they want is to see her miserable.* CINDERELLA *says nothing, but tries to obey her cruel sisters, holding back her tears while they torment her in this fashion.)*

CINDERELLA: All right sisters.

CHARLOTTE: Look at your hands! What dirt! Your hands are always dirty! Don't you ever look in the glass?

CINDERELLA: But you said I would be wasting my time in front of it.

DAISY: Never mind looking in the glass! Leave that kind of thing to us who are ladies. You can wash your face and hands without looking in the glass! Here, polish my shoes!

(The same nagging is repeated with even greater speed and heartlessness.)

CHARLOTTE: Tie up my ribbons!

DAISY: Lace me up!

CHARLOTTE: Fix my hair!

DAISY: Iron my petticoat!

CHARLOTTE AND DAISY: Paint my lips, my eyes, my cheeks!

DAISY: Polish my shoes!

CHARLOTTE: Trim my nails!

DAISY: Powder my nose!

DAISY AND CHARLOTTE: Hurry! Quick! Stir yourself! Move! Lazy good-for-nothing!

(They practically beat her off the scene to fetch their clothes. Having demonstrated their authority, they relax a few moments and sit down to fan themselves like two great ladies waiting to be served. CINDERELLA comes back, bringing in CHARLOTTE'S gown which she is planning to wear to the ball. She helps CHARLOTTE get into it, but of course nothing that she does pleases the haughty CHARLOTTE who, during the ceremony, taunts CINDERELLA with little, insulting remarks such as "clumsy fingers," "wait a minute," "not that way, stupid." DAISY helps by laughing and chuckling and saying inaudible nothings, all of which CINDERELLA takes very patiently. When CHARLOTTE is in her gown, CINDERELLA goes off to fetch DAISY'S. In the meantime CHARLOTTE struts about admiring herself, pulling here, arranging there, asking DAISY how she looks, and the other little things that easily occur to ladies. CINDERELLA then returns and the ceremony of dressing DAISY begins with very much the same procedure as in CHARLOTTE'S case. The two sisters can also help each other to dress. This whole scene should create an atmosphere of great excitement with CINDERELLA as the butt of all the unpleasant remarks. The two sisters are finally dressed and the scene continues.)

DAISY: Get the mirror, Cinderella.

(CINDERELLA fetches a large hand mirror which the sisters fight over to admire themselves in.)

DAISY: This velvet and lace ought to make the ball spin. I'm glad I didn't have a cloth-of-gold dress made.

CHARLOTTE: This diamond necklace and my gold-flowered cape will make eyes sparkle.

DAISY AND CHARLOTTE: It's such a relief to be rich.

CHARLOTTE: Wouldn't you like to go to the ball, Cinderella?

CINDERELLA: It's not for simple maids like me.

CHARLOTTE: You are right. The people would laugh at you.

DAISY: With your cinderish clothes.

CHARLOTTE: With your simple speech.

DAISY: And your ignorant ways. There will be handsome princes there.

CHARLOTTE: And elegant courtiers.

DAISY: And very fancy ladies.

CHARLOTTE: And music and dancing and singing and wooing.

DAISY: Wouldn't you like to go to the ball, Cinderella?

CINDERELLA: If you would let me wear one of your cast-off gowns, I would gladly go and just sit in a corner and look on.

DAISY AND CHARLOTTE: Ha, ha, ha! You are so funny, sister. You would be like a lost sparrow among birds of paradise. You would stop the ball.

(The coachman's trumpet is heard.)

STEPMOTHER'S VOICE: Hurry, hurry, girls! The coach is waiting for us!

DAISY: Come. We must go. The coach is waiting for us, sister.

CHARLOTTE: Good-by, Cinderella. We'll tell you all about it tomorrow.

CINDERELLA: Good-by, sisters, and good luck to you.

(The sisters make a great ado and bustle as they get ready to go off, for they want to make sure that they are leaving nothing behind. Their giggling and chattering are heard off stage, mingled with the STEPMOTHER'S *voice urging them to "Hurry up! Hurry!" Finally the sound of horses' hoofs and the coachman's whip and trumpet die out in the distance.* CINDERELLA *waves in the direction of the coach for a few moments. Then when all is very still she feels very lonely. She sits by the hearth and begins to sob with her face in her hands. She sobs and sobs until her sobs turn into words and she says—)*

CINDERELLA: I wish, I wish, I wish, I wish—

(There is a sound of jingling bells resembling sleigh bells at first from one point in the room, then another. CINDERELLA looks about her and listens. She then sobs once more with her face in her hands, continuing to say "I wish, I wish—" Suddenly the back of the hearth disappears like a sliding door, and the FAIRY GODMOTHER steps through it and comes on the stage, unseen by CINDERELLA. She touches CINDERELLA gently on the head with her wand. Then she makes a pirouette which sets all her bells a-jingling. CINDERELLA starts and beholds the FAIRY GODMOTHER standing over her.)

GODMOTHER: I know your wish, Cinderella. You wish that you, too, could go to the ball tonight. Is it not so?

CINDERELLA: Yes, I do wish it, godmother. But it isn't any use.

GODMOTHER: Who knows? Perhaps you will go. Miracles still happen. They still happen, child.

CINDERELLA: Oh, godmother, I would love to go to the ball. I want to see the Prince. They say he is very handsome. I want to see the million lights.

GODMOTHER: The Prince is very, very handsome. You may still dance with him.

CINDERELLA: Oh, godmother! My sisters have been talking about him and the court for weeks. I can just see everything.

GODMOTHER: Well, we shall see. Go into the garden, Cinderella, and bring me one of the large pumpkins.

CINDERELLA: Yes, godmother. *(She brings in the pumpkin.)*

GODMOTHER: Good! Now fetch the mousetrap and let us see what is in it.

CINDERELLA: Yes, godmother. *(She gets the mousetrap.)*

GODMOTHER: One, two, three, four, five, six nice plump little mice. Good! Just right! Now, Cinderella dear, hold your eyes so that they don't pop out of your head, for I

am going to do a little magic trick for you. Let us put
them all in a pot and then see what a porridge they will
make.

*(She takes the pumpkin and throws it off the stage. Then
she throws the mousetrap. These can be caught by someone
who is standing there ready. She then begins her incantation
—see below—making great circles with her wand and jingling
the bells. If possible the lights on the stage should go on and
off during the magic scene. When the incantation is all
finished a rather dim blue light should pervade the stage.
The neighing of horses and the cracking of a whip are heard.
Suddenly a huge shadow of the magic coach and horses is
thrown on the wall, through the open door. This can be
done with an electric bulb behind a cardboard cutout of the
coach and horses, held by someone in the wings at a proper
angle.)*

GODMOTHER: Golden pumpkin, little gray mice
　　　　　To Cinderella, please be nice.
　　　　　Shake and mix stones and sticks,
　　　　　Wood and tin, make a din
　　　　　Mix them up in twenty-two courses.
　　　　　Abracadabra, and candelabra,
　　　　　Pumpkin be coach and mice be horses!

CINDERELLA: Oh, godmother, how lovely!

(She claps her hands and dances for joy.)

GODMOTHER: Step in, little Cinderella! The coach is ready to
take you to the ball.

CINDERELLA: But look at these rags, godmother. How could
I go like this?

GODMOTHER: My, my! What a difficult child to please! Get
into that closet and count ten.

*(She lifts the end of the tablecloth that is farthest back-
stage and holds it over CINDERELLA's head.)*

CINDERELLA: One, two, three, four, five, six, seven, eight, nine, ten.

(While she is counting, substitute a dazzingly dressed Cinderella marionette. At the count of ten the GODMOTHER *jerks the tablecloth away and* CINDERELLA *appears in all her elegance. The horses whistle admiringly.)*

CINDERELLA: Oh, godmother, I feel so different.

GODMOTHER: You look a little different, dear. Step into the coach, now. You haven't much time to waste. Listen well and remember one thing, Cinderella. You must leave this ball before midnight, no matter what happens to detain you. If you remain one moment after midnight has struck, everything will vanish. The horses and coachman will change back to mice. The coach will turn to a pumpkin and your pretty dress will fall in rags about you. So keep your eye on the clock and listen carefully for the stroke of the hour.

CINDERELLA: I will remember, godmother dear, and I will leave in plenty of time. I can't thank you enough.

GODMOTHER: Never mind the thanks. Be full of joy at the ball and remember the clock. (CINDERELLA *goes out through the door and presumably gets inside the coach. The* GOD-MOTHER *then whips her wand, spins around so that all the bells jingle. The horses are heard neighing and soon they are trotting off in the distance.)* Giddap, my fine ones, giddap! Run! The cat is coming. Meow! Meow!

(And the curtain falls.)

SCENE TWO. *The ball room in the* PRINCE's *palace. It is brilliantly lighted with many colored lights hanging from the ceiling. Tall pillars go out of sight in the air. Festoons of colored paper and gold and silver tinsel cord make the room look very bright and gay. Before the curtain rises gay dance music and many voices laughing and talking are heard. The*

curtain rises and discloses ladies in beautiful gowns and cour-
tiers and young men dressed in many-colored costumes, danc-
ing around the pillars and making merry. The PRINCE *is*
dancing with DAISY *in the center of the floor.*

DAISY: You have such light feet, Prince. How you dance!

PRINCE: You have such a light head, lady. It doesn't wrinkle
my shoulder at all.

DAISY: Oh, thank you, Prince. It's nice music.

PRINCE: Yes. The music is very fine.

DAISY: Oh, thank you, Prince. We do agree so.

(*The music suddenly stops. While the* PRINCE *and* DAISY
are talking, the music and laughing should not stop, but in
order that the dialogue may be heard it should become sub-
dued, only to break forth again when the dialogue ceases for
a few seconds. Every time the music stops the guests should
form in careless groups, laugh, and chat.)

CHARLOTTE (*rushing up to the* PRINCE *and stepping between*
him and DAISY): Here I am, Prince. This is our dance.
You remember?

PRINCE: Oh, is it? I don't remember.

DAISY (*pushing her away*): But it hasn't started yet. The
Prince wishes to go in the garden for a few minutes.

CHARLOTTE: But the dance is about to begin.

DAISY: It isn't!

CHARLOTTE: It is!

DAISY: It isn't!

CHARLOTTE: It is!

DAISY: It isn't!

CHARLOTTE: It is!

(*As they quarrel they gradually push and pull each other*
off the stage, while the PRINCE, *amused, seeks refuge in the*
company of some other guests.)

(NERO, *the butler, enters and approaches the* PRINCE.)

NERO: Your Highness, a strange Princess has just arrived. Will you be so good as to receive her? She seems very shy but very regal.

PRINCE: Where did she come from?

NERO: She didn't say, your Highness. But I'm sure she is some remarkable princess. She arrived in a coach that is even grander than yours, if your Highness will pardon me. Her gown dazzles with jewels and her feet are like little glass doves.

PRINCE: Take me to her.

NERO: Your Highness!

(He bows and leads the PRINCE off the scene. The guests, as though attracted by this newcomer, all follow the PRINCE. CHARLOTTE and DAISY reenter still quarreling and still saying, "It is!" "It isn't!")

CHARLOTTE *(suddenly discovering the absence of the PRINCE)*: There, he's gone! You're so jealous, sister.

DAISY: You're too anxious, sister. But he'll come back. The music hasn't started yet.

CHARLOTTE: We'll see! I wonder if he has chosen his bride yet.

DAISY: Who knows? The night is still young. He said some nice things to me, about my head and things.

CHARLOTTE: Really? Could he have said the same thing to you as he said to me?

DAISY: Oh, no! Impossible! He's too true and loyal.

CHARLOTTE: Yes, yes. He couldn't have said to anybody else the pretty things he said to me.

DAISY AND CHARLOTTE: My Prince!

(Exclamations of wonder are heard off stage which attract the attention of DAISY and CHARLOTTE.)

CHARLOTTE *(getting a glimpse of CINDERELLA)*: Look, sister. A new lady has arrived.

DAISY: A grand lady! What jewels! What a manner!

CHARLOTTE: She is very pretty, too.

DAISY: Yes. She is beautiful. The Prince's lips seem to be glued to her hand. Look at her feet. Did you ever see such slippers? They must be made of crystal.

(*The music begins to play again and it seems to be a special number for the* PRINCE *and* CINDERELLA, *who presently appear on the stage, dancing together. The other guests follow, also dancing. All are very much impressed by* CINDERELLA *and whisper all sorts of compliments to each other such as:* "Isn't she magnificent!" "Unbelievable!" "Who is she?" "It looks like the Princess of the Moon." "What feet!" "Crystal without a doubt!" "They must be diamonds." "What a lovely face." "The Prince is smiling at last!" "At last!")

CHARLOTTE: There goes my dance. The Prince is dancing with the newcomer. See what you have done for me!

DAISY: Here he comes. Tell the Prince about it.

(*She goes off dancing with one of the guests.*)

CINDERELLA (*as she is dancing with the* PRINCE): Oh, Prince, you mustn't flatter me.

CHARLOTTE (*who is following the* PRINCE *around as he dances with* CINDERELLA): Oh, Prince, this is our dance. Don't you remember?

PRINCE (*who pays no heed whatsoever to* CHARLOTTE, *continues to* CINDERELLA): Your eyes are so blue, your hair is so soft, your hands are so small, and your feet are so precious.

CINDERELLA: Oh, thank you, Prince. But I'm really not what you think.

PRINCE: How is it that I have never seen you or heard of you before? (*Stops dancing for a moment.*) Who are you, Princess?

CINDERELLA: I'll tell you a little later, Prince. Let us dance now. You dance divinely.

PRINCE: Tell me who you are, my sweet Princess. I have been as one asleep, but now I am awake to life. What is your name?

CINDERELLA: I can't tell you now, Prince. I promise to tell you later.

CHARLOTTE: Prince, you promised the dance to me.

PRINCE: I hope the music never stops, Princess. You dance so well. *(They dance another turn or two and the music does stop.)* It will start again. Let us have some fruit. Nero! Bring fruit! I seem to have been waiting for you, strange Princess.

CINDERELLA: Oh, Prince. You are too good to me.

(NERO enters with a large tray of fruit. The clock begins to strike the hour of ten, the sound of which makes CINDERELLA start violently.)

PRINCE: Why do you start, strange Princess?

CINDERELLA: The clock has such a peculiar sound. *(Inviting her two stepsisters who do not recognize her in the least.)* Will you have some fruit, pretty ladies? Here are oranges and peaches and grapes.

DAISY AND CHARLOTTE: Oh, thank you, Princess. We would like some fruit.

(They take the fruit from the tray. NERO passes the tray among the other guests and finally goes off. The music starts again. The PRINCE turns to CINDERELLA.)

PRINCE: Come, Princess, let us dance.

CINDERELLA: Gladly, Prince.

DAISY: The Prince is dancing with her again.

CHARLOTTE: Lucky girl!

(CINDERELLA and the PRINCE appear and disappear among the guests. The clock begins to strike eleven. CINDERELLA stops dancing very suddenly and counts the strokes of the clock.)

CINDERELLA: Wait, Prince! One, two, three, four, five, six, seven, eight, nine, ten, eleven. I must leave, Prince. You must excuse me.

PRINCE: Nonsense, sweet Princess. The dance is only beginning.

CINDERELLA: I really must go. It is getting late.

PRINCE: But it is so early. When you leave, I will escort you home with a thousand torches. Come dance, strange Princess.

CINDERELLA: Only a little longer, Prince.

(CINDERELLA *is persuaded to dance, and the* PRINCE *whirls her off the scene. In a few seconds all the dancing couples disappear in the direction of the* PRINCE *and* CINDERELLA, *leaving the stage empty except for* DAISY *and* CHARLOTTE.)

CHARLOTTE: The Prince dances only with her.

DAISY: How she dances!

CHARLOTTE: Quite as well as the Prince himself.

(*The stepsisters sigh audibly.*)

NERO (*enters*): Will you give me the pleasure of a dance with you, madam?

CHARLOTTE: Oh, certainly. If it will give you much pleasure.

NERO: It will give me very much pleasure.

CHARLOTTE: With pleasure. (*They dance together.*)

NERO: Thank you, madam. (*To* DAISY): Will you do me the honor to dance with me, madam?

DAISY: Yes, yes. If you consider it such an honor.

NERO: Such a great honor.

DAISY: Honored. (*They dance.*)

NERO: This is the first real dance I've had tonight.

DAISY: The moon is lovely through the trees.

NERO: Oh, yes, it's a very pretty moon. Let us go and look at it.

(NERO *and* DAISY *go off followed by* CHARLOTTE, *leaving*

the stage completely empty. In a few seconds the music also stops and there is a moment of dead empty silence. Then the clock begins to strike the ominous midnight hour very slowly. At about the third stroke the quick little steps of CINDERELLA *are heard running toward the stage and she herself soon comes in looking very much frightened.)*

CINDERELLA: Oh, dear, oh dear, oh dear! I'll be lost! Where's the door? How do I get out? It must be down those stairs! Five, six, oh, dear! I clean forgot the time. Eight! Oh, dear! Oh, dear! Run! Run! Ten!

(During this speech she turns about this way and that way, not knowing where to run. She finally dashes off, and soon afterwards a great door is heard to slam just as the twelfth stroke is struck. The PRINCE, *who has been so suddenly deserted, rushes onto the scene, looking about and calling frantically.)*

PRINCE *(coming downstage and looking out over the audience as if seeking* CINDERELLA *in the distance)*: Princess! Princess! *(The music is playing rather softly. The guests slowly appear by ones and twos at the back of the scene, on tiptoes and whispering to each other as if sensing that something has happened.)* Princess! Princess! Wait! Wait! Oh, Princess! Where are you, Princess? My Princess! Where are you, Princess? Princess!

NERO *(dashing in)*: What is it, your Highness?

PRINCE: Where did the strange Princess go? She seemed to disappear.

NERO: I saw her go down those stairs, Prince.

PRINCE: Run! See if you can catch her.

NERO: Your Highness! *(And he bolts off.)*

NERO *(makes his return, carrying something very carefully in his hands. It is a glass slipper.)*: Your Highness.

PRINCE: Yes! Quick! Where is she?

NERO (*holding up the glass slipper*): This is the only trace I could find of her, Prince. The night is as still and empty as—as—could be. I found this at the foot of the stairs, jammed in the door, like a scrap of bone at the wolf's mouth.

PRINCE (*taking the slipper very affectionately*): Her slipper.

(*The guests in chorus*): A glass slipper!

PRINCE: Her tiny glass slipper.

(*The guests in chorus*): So tiny!

PRINCE: So small a slipper can only . . .

NERO: Fit the foot it belongs to.

PRINCE: Stop the music! Let the dancing cease. The ball is over.

NERO (*steps up to the middle of the stage, turns to the guests and says*): Good night!

    (*At this the guests vanish.*)

PRINCE: Nero, go to every mansion, cottage, and hut in the kingdom. Let every maid, rich and poor, try this slipper. I proclaim that she who can wear this slipper with ease shall be my wife, for she must be the strange princess. Start the search immediately.

NERO: Your Highness, immediately.

    (*The* PRINCE *makes his melancholy exit.* NERO *claps his hands and a* PAGE *with a silken cushion appears, followed by a drummer boy and a* PAGE *who carries a trumpet. The slipper is placed on the silken cushion.* NERO *indicates the direction and they file off the scene, beating the drum and blowing the trumpet. The curtain falls.*)

    SCENE THREE *is exactly the same as* SCENE ONE. CHARLOTTE *and* DAISY *are still in their ball gowns and are sitting dejectedly at the table.* CINDERELLA *is in her fated corner with the cinders, but she has thoughts of her own.*

CHARLOTTE: Poor Prince!

DAISY: Poor, poor Prince.

DAISY AND CHARLOTTE: Poor Prince.

DAISY: Aren't you sorry for the Prince, Cinderella?

CINDERELLA: I don't know, I didn't see the Princess.

DAISY: That's right, you unlucky maid. She was so beautiful, Cinderella, and so kind and generous.

CHARLOTTE: She gave us oranges and peaches.

DAISY: And how she could dance! The Prince would dance with no one else.

CHARLOTTE: Poor Prince. If he doesn't find her, he will surely die.

DAISY: They say he hasn't slept a wink.

CHARLOTTE: Not a wink! Poor Prince! Aren't you sorry for him, Cinderella?

DAISY: Your heart must be like those cinders you sit in.

CINDERELLA: I am very sorry for the Prince.

CINDERELLA, DAISY AND CHARLOTTE: Poor Prince.

(A drum and a trumpet are heard in the distance. At the sound the two stepsisters rush to the door.)

CHARLOTTE: The coach with the little glass slipper is coming.

DAISY: Hurry!

CHARLOTTE: Wash your feet!

DAISY: New stockings!

CHARLOTTE: Perfume!

DAISY: Cinderella, quick!

CHARLOTTE: I have fasted ever since that night to make my feet smaller.

DAISY: I have squeezed my feet a dozen times a day.

CHARLOTTE: Tidy up the place!

DAISY: They are outside the door.

(The heralds of the slipper are heard drawing nearer and nearer. In this scene somewhat the same confusion and helter-

*skelter bustle takes place as in the first scene when the sisters
are getting ready for the ball.)*
CHARLOTTE: This must be the very next house.
DAISY: I still have hope, sister.
CHARLOTTE: I, too, sister.
DAISY: Hurry! Hurry!

    *(A chorus of voices burst into song just outside the door.
They sing the song of the little glass slipper, which has caused
the Prince so much joy and pain):*
    A tiny crystal slipper
    Tumbled out of the sky,
    Out of the dipper
    Into the Prince's eye.
    Love is blind.
    Blind in one eye.
    Look, search, seek, find
    Its mate by and by
    Slipper, slipper, crystal boot,
    Gallop, fly, and find the foot.

    *(The drum and trumpet are heard once more as the
prelude to the entrance of the* PAGE. *His proclamation is
punctuated with the beating of the drum as was his previous
announcement in the first scene.)*
PAGE *(outside)*: It is the royal wish of his Highness, the Prince
    of the kingdom, of the King, of his obedient, loyal and
    humble subjects, that every maid in the mentioned king-
    dom who has feet on the legs of her body should try, essay,
    or otherwise endeavor to fit the little glass slipper that was
    left behind in the mysterious midnight flight of the foot.
    The next maid, matron, mademoiselle, or signorina will
    now do the slipper the courtesy to endeavor to effect an
    entrance.

    (At the conclusion of the speech NERO *enters followed*

by the bearer of the glass slipper, who in turn is followed by the little PAGE *who beats the drum and the one who blows the trumpet.)*

DAISY: Here is my foot.

NERO: The slipper.

(The drummer beats the drum and the other page blows the horn. The slipper bearer puts down the silken cushion with the slipper and DAISY *comes forward to try her luck.)*

DAISY *(puffing and pulling)*: This is a funny slipper. The harder I press the smaller it seems to get. I'm all tired out and my foot is still half on the outside.

NERO: If you are satisfied of the unfitness, madam, allow the next one to try.

DAISY: My sister, try your fortune. I'll be a cripple if I try any more.

CHARLOTTE *(going through the same performance, using every means in her power to force the foot into the slipper)*: It shrinks! It doesn't stretch! It seems to have teeth that bite the foot! Ouch!

NERO: Next!

DAISY: No one else in this house, Mr. Page.

NERO: No other maidens in this house? Look well! Seek! Search! Investigate!

DAISY AND CHARLOTTE: We are the only maidens in the house, Mr. Page.

NERO: Let us depart to the next house.

(The glass slipper procession starts to go, then NERO *changes his mind and stops. Through this whole performance of trying the slipper* CINDERELLA *has been hidden from sight by the table which the sisters have carefully pushed toward the fireplace early in the scene so that the maid in rags may not be seen.)*

NERO: Are you sure there are no other maidens in this house?

I have a peculiar feeling—an odd, queer, funny, obstinate feeling—funny.

DAISY AND CHARLOTTE: No one else, Mr. Page.

CINDERELLA: Excepting poor me!

NERO: Ah, ha! Where is that voice?

CINDERELLA: Over here. Next to the cinders.

(DAISY *and* CHARLOTTE *go toward the spot where* CINDER- ELLA *is sitting and make various gestures to keep her quiet and out of sight.*)

CHARLOTTE: She's just Cinderella.

DAISY: She doesn't count.

NERO: Cinder or corn whiskers! My orders are my commands! If the maid has a foot, she shall try the slipper!

CINDERELLA: I have two feet.

DAISY: It's an insult to the Prince. She is all covered with ashes. She has no education or fine manners or elegant speech.

NERO: My orders are to look for feet and nothing else. *(He pushes the stepsisters out of the way and helps* CINDERELLA *to her feet.)* Young maiden, will your foot do the slipper the courtesy?

CINDERELLA: Gladly, Mr. Page.

NERO: The slipper!

(*The drum and trumpet play, and with no effort at all* CINDERELLA's *foot slips into the glass slipper.)*

CHARLOTTE: What an insult!

DAISY: What an affront!

CHARLOTTE: What an affront!

DAISY: What an insult!

NERO: Look, it fits! How very easily it fits!

DAISY AND CHARLOTTE: What! It fits?

CINDERELLA: It does fit. I knew it would fit.

CHARLOTTE: How disgraceful!

DAISY: How shocking!

PAGE *(in great wonder at the sight of the two glass slippers on* CINDERELLA's *feet, for* CINDERELLA *has been wearing the other slipper and hiding it very carefully all the time)*: And what is that other one?

CINDERELLA: Oh, that's the lost slipper's mate that I wore at the ball.

(They all crowd about CINDERELLA, *the* PAGE, *the drummer, and the stepsisters, eager to have a glimpse of the impossible, exclaiming all at the same time: "Its mate!" "It fits!" "Two glass slippers!" "At the ball!" "Ah!")*

NERO *(with loud authority)*: Silence! *(Goes to the door and proclaims his information to those waiting outside.)* It fits! It fits! Let all the kingdom hear that it fits!

(Chorus of off-stage voices): It fits! It fits!

NERO *(still in the door)*: His Highness, the Prince, may step out of the coach and enter, for this is the house where the little glass slipper abides and fits. *(The trumpet and drums hail the* PRINCE.) The Prince!

PRINCE *(enters to music and goes straight to* CINDERELLA *and kisses her hand)*: Sweet princess of the crystal slippers, I know you now without your fine gown.

CHARLOTTE: But, your Highness, she is Cinderella, princess of the cinders.

DAISY: There in the fireplace!

PRINCE: Cinderella! What a celestial name! Angels have fallen from the sky in the form of burning cinders. Could anyone be more a princess than the princess of these angels? Come into my coach, Princess Cinderella.

CINDERELLA: Gladly, Prince. Good-by for the present, sisters. I'll send for you at court. Don't be angry with me if my foot had the impudence to fit the slipper when yours would not.

DAISY AND CHARLOTTE: We are so happy for you, sister! So very happy! (*The* PRINCE *leads* CINDERELLA *out to the coach. The rest of the entourage follow, winding up with the* PAGE, *who blows his trumpet, and the drummer who beats his drum. As soon as the royal procession is past the door, the two sisters begin to stamp, wrangle, and tear their hair at their misfortune and* CINDERELLA'S *good fortune. But the song of the crystal slipper outside drowns their voices*):

A tiny crystal slipper
Tumbled out of the sky,
Out of the dipper
Into the Prince's eye.
Love is blind,
Blind in one eye.
Look, search, seek, find
Its mate by and by.
Slipper, slipper, crystal boot,
Gallop, fly and find the foot.

(*Curtain*)

PINOCCHIO

A PLAY IN THREE ACTS

—<✶>—

Characters

GEPPETTO

PINOCCHIO

BLUE FAIRY

WICK

In addition there is the POLICEMAN, the CRICKET, the PIE-MAN, the INNKEEPER, CHICKEN, COALMAN, BRICKLAYER, FRANKFURTER MAN, BOY, COACHMAN, DONKEY, DORMOUSE, COOK, MR. BILLY and the people of the circus, and off-stage voices.

PINOCCHIO

THIS, of course, is a very elaborate play, done with quite a large cast and scenes and properties. We give the play as is, but, if you feel it may be too much for you, you can just follow the bare outline and make shortcuts. Use the same marionettes to portray the various characters by slightly changing their costumes. Use the same sets for different scenes with little changes. Adapt the action to fit your needs and facilities—or even do one section of it.

If you're in doubt about any of the technical points that the play brings up, we refer you back to the staging of plays section of the book where all this is explained.

ACT I

SCENE ONE. GEPPETTO's *cottage. Plain white or yellow walls with one window and a door. A rough kitchen table, which* GEPPETTO *uses as a workbench. A stool and two or three other objects complete the furniture. There is a basin of water standing on the floor to one side of the stage.*

(As the curtain rises, GEPPETTO *is chopping away at the block, which has already acquired the shape of* PINOCCHIO's *head. The nose should be arranged so that it can be lengthened and shortened by sliding it in and out, as this is an important part of the action.)*

GEPPETTO *(singing)*:
    Carve, carve, carve.
    As I starve, starve, starve.

But now that I am an artist I shouldn't mind so much going hungry. Wait, Geppetto, this is going to make your fortune. Won't you? *(Addressing the block.)* You wicked little eyes, what are you looking at?

I don't like your nose. It should be longer. *(He carves.)* Goodness, it is growing like a mushroom! *(He cuts, and as he turns his head it grows again.)* What's that? What's that? I cut it away and it still grows.

(The nose persists in growing a little longer each time he cuts.)

As I cut, it grows, and as it grows, I cut. At this rate it will have to remain the same length.

(He hums a tune.)

What name should I give this masterpiece of mine?

(He thinks hard, scrutinizing the head and mumbling inaudible names to himself.)

I know! I know! I'll call him Pinocchio. Pinocchio! Pinocchio! Pinocchio! It's a very lucky name. Once I knew a whole family of Pinocchios. There was Pinocchio, the father. There was Pinocchio, the mother, and there were all the little Pinocchinos, any number of them. And they were all lucky. The luckiest of them was a successful beggar. You shall be named Pinocchio. And now, my Pinocchio, I shall give you a mouth, for without a mouth you could not talk.

(He carefully carves out the mouth, which breaks out into giggling as soon as it is finished.) There!

Now I shall make your arms. You must have arms; hands at the very least. Here is one arm for you. *(He hums a tune.)* I suppose you really ought to have another. One would probably be overworked.

(As he works and sings with his eyes glued to what he is doing, PINOCCHIO's finished hand slaps him on the head.)

Mamma mia! Is the ceiling falling? No, it's still up there. Where did that come from?

(He looks about, and as he does so the hand slaps him on the back.)

Ouch! Ouch! This place must be haunted.

(He looks again about himself and then looks hard at PINOCCHIO *with some suspicion. He pretends to look away again and turns back quickly to catch* PINOCCHIO *with his arm raised ready to strike again. Not knowing what to do,* PINOCCHIO *feigns to be scratching his head.)*

Ah! Ah! So it's you? You wooden imp! Take this!

(He slaps PINOCCHIO, *who begins to cry.)*

Let that keep you out of mischief while I finish your legs.

*(*GEPPETTO *sings and carves away, while* PINOCCHIO *continues to cry louder and louder.)*

Stop crying! Stop crying, I said! Look! Look! Your left leg. Do you like it?

*(*PINOCCHIO, *seeing his leg, forgets his crying and giggles, only to be mimicked by* GEPPETO.)

You dear little scoundrel, you are so tough, you've dulled my best hatchet.

(As GEPPETTO *turns away to sharpen the hatchet* PINOCCHIO *kicks him.)*

You little imp. Why, you are not even finished yet—and —well, of all the—already you begin to show such disrespect for your father. It's enough to—I don't know what we are coming to—It's like a—Well, there is only one thing to do—I shan't finish you, that's all. You don't deserve to be finished. And—and—I don't think I will finish you. I'm finished—

*(*PINOCCHIO *cries bitterly.)*

No use, lad! No use!

*(*PINOCCHIO *cries more bitterly.)*

Cry all you like. Shed tears! If you shed enough you'll float away on them.

(PINOCCHIO *begins to scream.*)

That's bad, my boy. Bad! Bad! To show such disrespect when you are only fifty-per-cent boy. What would you do if—I don't even dare to think about it—No! Stay as you are.

(PINOCCHIO *screams even more loudly.*)

Don't scream so loudly! The neighbors will think that I am beating someone.

(PINOCCHIO *continues to scream.*)

Don't scream! Oh, why did I make that mouth!

(PINOCCHIO *cries.*)

Of course if you are really sorry, I might forgive you.

(PINOCCHIO *stops crying.*)

Are you sorry you did what you did?

(PINOCCHIO *nods.*)

In that case I will finish you.

(PINOCCHIO *laughs and kicks his legs wildly as he sits on the table.*)

PINOCCHIO: Hurray! Hurray! Hurray!

GEPPETTO: Not so gay, my lad, not so gay. You are not quite finished. You still must get your education.

PINOCCHIO: How?

GEPPETTO: You must go to school for that.

PINOCCHIO: School—school—school. I don't know why, but I don't like that name.

GEPPETTO: You will get used to it. Many learn to love it.

PINOCCHIO: What is it? Where is it? Is it something to eat? Give it to me. I will eat it all at once, and that's all.

GEPPETTO: Eat! That's necessary too, my boy. School is not exactly something to eat. Among other things it teaches you how to get something to eat.

PINOCCHIO: Will it teach me how to get a lot to eat?

GEPPETTO: That depends on how much you can learn, or how little.

PINOCCHIO: Oh! What else do they teach?

GEPPETTO: Something even better.

PINOCCHIO: Better?

GEPPETTO: Reading, writing and arithmetic.

PINOCCHIO: Um . . .

GEPPETTO: What are you thinking about, son?

PINOCCHIO: I am just wondering if all that was necessary.

GEPPETTO: Not only necessary, but compulsory, for one who wants to be a learned man.

PINOCCHIO: Does a learned man sing and dance? Does he juggle with a hundred balls at once and—and—a lot of things like that?

GEPPETTO: What are you thinking of, lad? Where did you get such ideas? Such nonsense! What put that in your head?

PINOCCHIO: I don't know. It must have rained in, I guess. I just thought that's what learned men do. Because if they do, I want to be a learned man.

GEPPETO: Son, son! Learned men are—they do—they are much wiser—this world is a serious place. When you are a learned man you will see for yourself. You will begin by going to school.

PINOCCHIO: But I can't go to school.

GEPPETTO: And why not?

PINOCCHIO: Because—well, because—because!

GEPPETO: Because you have to go.

PINOCCHIO: Because I haven't got any book.

GEPPETTO: Oh, yes, you have. A very nice book. And do you know how I got it? I had to sell my best coat to get you this book. My best coat! Now I haven't got any. But you will be able to go to school.

PINOCCHIO: Nope.

GEPPETO: And why not?

PINOCCHIO: Because I have no clothes?

GEPPETTO: But maybe that has been taken care of too, my lad. In fact I'm quite sure that it has. Let us see how well your good fairy has provided for you.

PINOCCHIO: Hurray, hurray, hurray! Please, Pappy, hurry up and put them on me!

GEPPETTO: Let's go take a peek and see what your good fairy left for you.

(PINOCCHIO *giggles and obeys.* GEPPETTO *carries* PINOCCHIO *to the closet and they enter it. You must work fast at this point. Have an assistant hand you an identical* PINOCCHIO *puppet dressed in a quaint jacket made of a material that looks like wall paper; a pair of black or brown pants that end above the knee, a white ruff, which may be attached to the jacket, and a white pointed cap. For his feet a pair of canvas shoes equipped with wooden soles would answer as well as anything.*)

GEPPETTO (*is heard admiring*): How well they fit! Now your hands. Turn around. Stand still. Down. Up. Now this way. Not this way; this way. Up. Up. Now for your hat. Look at it. Still now.

(*They come out and go back to the table where* GEPPETTO *takes the hatchet and appears to nail the hat on* PINOCCHIO'S *wooden head.*)

PINOCCHIO: Ouch!

GEPPETTO: Now here we have our little man. Let us look at him—our little wooden man. Magnificent! If you had crawled from under a glass case you couldn't have been any spicker. Walk over to that tub of water and look at yourself.

(PINOCCHIO *remains still.*)

Well, walk!

PINOCCHIO: Walk? How do you walk?

GEPPETTO: Of course *(chuckling gayly)* I forgot that you haven't learned to walk yet. We will begin right now. Watch me. Watch me now. One, two, three.

(GEPPETTO takes a few slow steps for PINOCCHIO's instruction.)

See? Now give me your hand and do the same.

(GEPPETTO leads PINOCCHIO around the room.)

One, two, three. Fine! One, two, three. Excellent! One, two, three. Again. One, two, three. One, two, three.

(GEPPETTO releases PINOCCHIO's hand and lets him walk all by himself while he marks time with his hands. PINOCCHIO continues to walk to the count. His speed gains with each lap around the table until he is running. He suddenly stops at the door, looks out and giggles with a grand idea.)

One, two, three. One, two, three. One, two, three. One, two, three. One, two, three. One, two, three. One, two, three.

(PINOCCHIO dashes into the street. The old man is so busy counting that he does not see PINOCCHIO. He continues to beat time still thinking that PINOCCHIO is taking his walking lesson.)

One, two, three. One—

(GEPPETTO suddenly looks up and sees neither PINOCCHIO nor his shadow.)

Where are you? Where is he? Pinocchio! Where are you? Pinocchio!

(The wooden feet of PINOCCHIO are heard pattering in the distance. GEPPETTO looks out the door.)

By the crooked back of a pink-eyed lizard, the little rascal has run off. Pinocchio! Pinocchio! Come back! Stop him! Stop him! Police! Police!

(GEPPETTO pursues PINOCCHIO, leaving his door ajar.

His distressed voice continues shouting as the curtain comes down.)

SCENE TWO *is a street with many houses on it. The houses may be represented by screens covered with wrapping or other paper with doors, windows, peaked roofs, and lamp posts drawn or painted on them. As the curtain rises a* POLICEMAN *is seen strutting to and fro on his beat. He is dressed in a blue uniform which makes him look like an admiral. He has brass buttons, glittering epaulets, a wide belt with a brass buckle, and a long curved sword hanging from it. He should have a large and curling mustache. His hat is very tall with a red pompon stuck in it. In the distance* PINOCCHIO's *pattering feet and* GEPPETTO's *shouting are heard.*

GEPPETTO *(off-stage)*: Stop him! Stop him! Policeman! Policeman!

Noises from crowd off-stage: Look! Oh, oh look! New circus freak! What's loose? Clear the way! Jumping Jack come to life!

POLICEMAN *(perceiving* PINOCCHIO, *who is still off-stage)*: Ah! What's this! What's that! Where is it? What's all this about?

GEPPETTO *(off-stage)*: Stop him! Stop him!

POLICEMAN: It's coming this way. We must be brave. *(He plants himself in the middle of the street.)* Stop in the name of the law!

PINOCCHIO *(runs into* POLICEMAN*)*: Let me go! Let me go!

POLICEMAN: Who are you? What are you? Where do you come from? Where are you going? Keep quiet in the name of the law!

(He holds PINOCCHIO *by the nose as* PINOCCHIO *tries to answer each question.)*

GEPPETTO *(entering out of breath)*: He belongs to me, Mr. Policeman. Thank you for catching him. He ran away.

POLICEMAN: Oh! He belongs to you. Then that is different. Then the law gives him up to you.

GEPPETTO: Come here, you little ruffian. Run away, will you? Do you think you can escape school that way? Well, you see you can't. See that policeman there, he'll always be waiting to catch you wherever you are. (*To the* POLICE-MAN.) Won't you?

(POLICEMAN *coughs.*)

GEPPETTO: He'll put you in another kind of school. Won't you?

(POLICEMAN *coughs.*)

GEPPETTO: For the present take this sound cuff on the ear. (*Looks for* PINOCCHIO's *ears.*) Oh, I forgot to make ears. And you may consider yourself very lucky. But just wait until we get home. Come along now! March!

PINOCCHIO: No, I won't go home. I don't want to go home. You'll spank me. Oh, please, Mr. Policeman, don't let him take me. He'll beat me. He's a wicked old man. Oh please, Mr. Policeman, he did it once before. He'll chop me to pieces.

POLICEMAN: Oh well, that's different. You, whatever your name is, old man. What is your name?

GEPPETTO: Geppetto, Mr. Policeman.

POLICEMAN: Oho! Geppetto! Oho! You are under arrest for intending to whip, beat, mutilate, or otherwise injure this thing—whatever it is. Come along!

GEPPETTO: But, your excellency, it's not true.

POLICEMAN: You mean that I'm a liar? Whether it is true or not, what's the difference. If I say come along, come along. As for you, whatever you are, continue to run. The law gives you the right of way. (*To* GEPPETTO.) Come along!

(POLICEMAN *pushes* GEPPETTO *before him.*)

GEPPETTO: Ungrateful child!

POLICEMAN: Move!

PINOCCHIO: Don't believe him.

GEPPETTO: To think I worked so hard to make a fine marionette of him.

PINOCCHIO: Don't believe him!

POLICEMAN: Move, move! (*Still pushing* GEPPETTO.)

GEPPETTO: Serves me right. I should have thought of it.

PINOCCHIO: Take him away:

POLICEMAN: I said move! In the name of the law, move!

(POLICEMAN *gives* GEPPETTO *a final push and exits.*)

PINOCCHIO: I am free! I am free! Free! Free! Free! No more dada to bother me! No one to make me go to school! Dada is going to jail and they ought to keep him there twenty or thirty years for treating me like this. It's wonderful to be alone with no one to bother me. Free! Free! Free!

CRICKET (*who has slowly come onto the stage during* PINOCCHIO's *last speech*): Cri! Cri! Cri!

(*The* CRICKET's *costume may be effectively made with a tight-fitting black or brown suit with two large buckram or cardboard wings painted green and gold. For the head a hat frame, which comes down over the eyes, also painted green.*)

PINOCCHIO: What was that? That must have been my echo! Free! Free! Free!

CRICKET: Cri! Cri! Cri!

PINOCCHIO (*trembling*): Was that my echo? It didn't sound just the same.

CRICKET: Cri! Cri! Cri! Pinocchio!

PINOCCHIO: Oh my! That sounded like my name.

CRICKET: Pinocchio!

PINOCCHIO: Oh!

CRICKET: Pinocchio!

PINOCCHIO: I had better run.

CRICKET: Pinocchio! You'll fall if you run! Better stay a little while! Cri—cri—cri! (PINOCCHIO *looks about, but does not see the* CRICKET.) Here I am, Pinocchio! Cri—cri—cri—cri!

PINOCCHIO (*seeing the* CRICKET): Who are you, I should like to know!

CRICKET: Cri, cri! I am the talking cricket.

PINOCCHIO: What do you want?

CRICKET: I want to talk to you. Cri—cri—cri! I have lived in your father's house for more than a hundred years.

PINOCCHIO: Really? Well, from now on, that house is mine and I want you to stay out of it.

CRICKET: Very well. I have left it already, for when mischief enters a house I clear out. Now I am going to tell you what you think and then I am going to tell you what you ought to know.

PINOCCHIO: Oh! Is that so? You had better hurry with your speech, I haven't got much time to waste here.

CRICKET: You think that this world is a circus, but it is not. You have just tumbled into it like a clown. But now that you are here, you must walk upright.

PINOCCHIO: Like a cricket?

CRICKET: Yes, like a cricket.

PINOCCHIO: And now what else?

CRICKET: Bad luck comes to youngsters who run away from home. You had better go back home, and repent, repent, repent.

PINOCCHIO: I am not going back home, because if I do, I shall have to go to school like all the other unhappy boys. I don't want to go to school, for if you go to school you can't run after wagons and you can't climb trees and you can't hunt birds' nests.

CRICKET: Truly your head is made of a block of wood, a block of wood, a block of wood!

PINOCCHIO: Shut up, you ugly insect! Don't wish me any bad
luck!

CRICKET: If you go to school you will learn a useful trade and
grow up into a useful, respectable, law-abiding citizen.

PINOCCHIO: Useful for what?

CRICKET: Useful for what? For what! Useful to be used. All
useful things are used. You will be used, in the scheme of
things. A useful trade can always be used.

PINOCCHIO: My dear Mr. Cricket, there is only one trade that
I like, but they don't teach it in your school.

CRICKET: All the trades are taught in school. Which one is
that?

PINOCCHIO: The best one in the world. Eating, sleeping, and
playing all day long. That's what I call a good trade.

CRICKET: You will come to a bad end—a very bad end.

PINOCCHIO: Be careful. This is the second time you have
wished me bad luck, the third time—look out!

CRICKET: Cri—cri—cri! Poor Pinocchio! Poor Pinocchio!

PINOCCHIO: Why, Mr. Cricket?

CRICKET: Because you are a marionette, but, worse yet, because your head is made of wood, wood, wood.

PINOCCHIO: You chattering insect! *(Goes to kick the* CRICKET,
who vanishes.) You better take to the air. Insects have no
business on earth, anyway.

CRICKET *(from off-stage)*: Wood, wood, wood.

(The POLICEMAN *walks across the stage, glaring at* PINOC-
CHIO, *who trembles until the terrifying uniform is once more
out of sight. The* PIEMAN *is heard crying his wares in the distance. He enters. The* PIEMAN *is dressed in white like a baker.
His white cook's cap is trimmed with bells. He has a white
ruff around his neck also trimmed with bells. His coat has
bells instead of buttons. The bottom of his apron is also
trimmed with bells. His piecard can be an oblong box stand-*

*ing on end, with two wheels trimmed with bells. Every move-
ment he makes sets the bells to jingling.)*

PIEMAN: Pies, pies, pies!

      Hot, pies, cold pies!

      Large pies, small pies!

      Take a look, fill your eyes,

      Taste them, delicious pies!

PINOCCHIO: Oh! I am hungry.

PIEMAN: Ah, a customer! I am at the service of hungry ones.
What size will you have, young gentleman?

PINOCCHIO: I could eat the largest you have, Mr. Pieman.

PIEMAN: Good! That will be just three cents. Three cents,
please!

PINOCCHIO: Oh! I didn't know one had to pay for them.

PIEMAN: Three cents, please.

PINOCCHIO: But I haven't got them now. Can't I pay you
sometime?

PIEMAN: Oh certainly. Sometime will be all right. Any time,
if you are here, five years from now you will find me. Any
time will do. Let me deliver it to you sometime. Pies! Pies!
Pies! Large pies! Fill your eyes!

    (He wheels his cart off, jingling the bells as he goes.)

PINOCCHIO: I am hungrier than ever now. I wish a table would
grow before me, with all kinds of pies, roast chicken, macaroni, with juicy red sauce, and a great big dish of ice cream
in all colors.

    *(At this point a table seems to walk out of the inn and
sets itself in front of* PINOCCHIO. *This can be done with a
plain board held on a stick from below. A round little man
who is the* INNKEEPER *is dressed in a chocolate-brown suit
looking a little like a headwaiter, with winged collar and
black tie. The coat has long tails. He has a shiny bald head.
His voice is high and piping.)*

PINOCCHIO: A table. Wonder if he heard me. *(Approaches and looks longingly at the table.)*

INNKEEPER: Good morning, young gentleman. I hope you have a good appetite. If you have, I am the doctor for you. Won't you sit down?

(PINOCCHIO *sits down on a stool which the* INNKEEPER *has placed for him. He reads the menu to* PINOCCHIO.)

Spinach a l'olio.

Roast duck stuffed with chestnuts.

Watercress salad.

Macaroni with beans, royal style, special.

Macaroni any style.

Ice cream, any kind, or anything else you would like.

PINOCCHIO: I want them all.

(POLICEMAN *once more makes his appearance, much to* PINOCCHIO's *discomfort. He eyes* PINOCCHIO *suspiciously, strokes his mustache and slowly walks off.)*

INNKEEPER: With pleasure, with pleasure. That will only cost you two gold pieces.

PINOCCHIO: Oh! But I have no money right now. I am only starting out to make my fortune. But I will be back.

INNKEEPER: I see, I see. *(Disappears.)*

(The INNKEEPER *quickly goes back into the inn to return almost immediately with a solitary egg, which he places before* PINOCCHIO. *Then, turning on his heel, he makes his exit in silence once more.)*

PINOCCHIO: An egg. I'll start with it anyway. *(He breaks the egg and out of the shell hops a little* CHICKEN, *peeping volubly. A hole in the top of the table through which the person underneath can thrust a little chick on a wire is a simple solution for this trick. The same person can also speak for the* CHICKEN.)

CHICKEN: Peep, peep, peep, Pinocchio. How do you do?

Thank you for saving me the trouble of breaking through the shell all by myself. I hope we shall meet again sometime. Regards from the family!

(With the conclusion of the CHICKEN'S *speech a nightmare suddenly descends on* PINOCCHIO. *The lights about him change and go off and on many times. The* CHICKEN *disappears. The* CRICKET *flies past laughing. The* PIEMAN *is heard calling his wares. The* POLICEMAN *walks past* PINOCCHIO *coughing. The* INNKEEPER *picks up the table and disappears with it like a flash. Drums are heard beating in the distance. This confusion dies down and* PINOCCHIO *is left all alone in the quiet street.)*

PINOCCHIO: Perhaps I did wrong to run away. I must be wrong. I shouldn't have caused my father to be locked up. He sold his only coat to buy me a reader. Poor dada. Pinocchio, you deserve not to eat. It's a terrible pain to be hungry. You had better turn over a new leaf—right away. I will begin to go to school today, and learn to read. Tomorrow I shall learn to write. And the next tomorrow I shall learn to count. Then with that education I shall go out and earn my fortune. With my first million dollars I'll buy a new coat for my dear dada, all made of wool. No, not wool—not even silk, it must be a coat all made of silver and gold, with diamond buttons. He deserves it. If it wasn't for him, I could never be a great man. Oh, dear dada, I am so sorry for what I have done. Just wait.

(Curtain)

ACT II

SCENE ONE.

PINOCCHIO: I'm getting hungrier and hungrier.

(He feels his pockets.)

If I had just one of those gold pieces I could—gee!
(Some people pass by.)
I wonder if these people would give me some pennies.
(A COALMAN *passes, carrying two bags of coal on his back.)*
(To the COALMAN*):* Will you please, mister, give me a few pennies? I'm hungry and I'm all alone and I haven't got anything—please, mister!

COALMAN *(he puts his bags down):* What's that? Pennies? You're hungry? That's too bad. You must be healthy. Sure, I'll give you ten cents if you help me carry one of these bags.

PINOCCHIO: Me? Carry that bag? I'm not a donkey, and I've never been one.

COALMAN: Such pride! I believe you're a rich little man in disguise. Try eating some of your pride if you are hungry.
(He picks up his bags and goes off. A BRICKLAYER *passes by.)*

PINOCCHIO *(to the* BRICKLAYER*):* Mister, can you please give me a penny or two? I'm so hungry, I'm yawning. *(He yawns.)*

BRICKLAYER: Well, well! That's not right. Young people shouldn't stay hungry for very long. Do you like ham? Cheese? Eggs? Fruit? Pie? Candy?
*(*PINOCCHIO *nods after each item.)*
Good! Come along with me. I need someone to hand me bricks while I lay them in place. You can earn enough money to buy all those good things.

PINOCCHIO: Oh, I can't do that.

BRICKLAYER: Why not?

PINOCCHIO: I can't—I—Those bricks are too heavy for me.

BRICKLAYER: Oh, I see; you're not hungry. If you're not

hungry that's different. You're just yawning to fool me.
Yawn away!

(*He goes off.* PINOCCHIO *yawns in desperation. A vendor
with a little frankfurter cart enters calling his wares.*)

FRANKFURTER MAN: Frankfurter—r—r—r—rs. American
frankfurters. Five cents apiece! Five, five, five, five cents.
Frankfurters. American frankfurters. Get 'em hot—hot—
hot—hot—hot—hot! Red hot, hot, hot!

(PINOCCHIO's *eyes nearly pop out at the sight and he
approaches the vendor.*)

PINOCCHIO: Please, mister, can I have one? I'm hungry and I
have no money, and no father and no mother. Please,
mister!

FRANKFURTER MAN: Hot, hot, hot, hot, hot! Sure I'll give
you one. Here, first take these two pots and go and wash
them for me and bring back a bundle of sticks for my
little stove.

PINOCCHIO: Who? Me? I'm not a servant.

FRANKFURTER MAN: Oh, so you're a gentleman. All right.
You can follow me and pick up the crumbs that my cus-
tomers drop—if you are quicker than the birds. Hot! Hot!
Hot! Red hot!

(*He goes off and some boys come in who eye* PINOCCHIO
with mischievous intentions.)

ONE BOY: Look, look, look!

(*They whisper to each other and laugh.*)

ANOTHER BOY: Is that right, you're hungry?

PINOCCHIO: And what if I am?

BOYS: Ha, ha, ha, ha! And what if he is! Let's help him
out.

You like pie, don't you? Let's feed him some mud pies.
Open your mouth and see how many you can catch.

(*They throw mud and stones at* PINOCCHIO, *who tries to
dodge them, weeping with rage. He defends himself as best*

he can, kicking right and left with his wooden feet, which do succeed in putting one or two of his tormentors out of the game. But he is one and they are many, so he gets the worst of it. In the midst of the fray the BLUE FAIRY, *dressed as a peasant woman, comes to* PINOCCHIO's *rescue. She is carrying two jugs of water. She shoos the urchins off and finally scatters them by throwing water over them.* PINOCCHIO *puts his face down on the wall and weeps over his ill fortune. The* BLUE FAIRY *pats him gently on the back.)*

BLUE FAIRY: Never mind. Never mind. They really didn't hurt you.

PINOCCHIO *(eyes the water jugs thirstily)*: Please, lady, may I please have a drink?

BLUE FAIRY: Of course, lad. Drink all you can hold.

*(*PINOCCHIO *drinks his fill. He puts down the jug with a long and regretful sigh.)*

PINOCCHIO: Now I'm not thirsty any more. But I'm still hungry, even more than before—and I wish I wasn't.

BLUE FAIRY: Did you say you were hungry, lad?

*(*PINOCCHIO *nods.)*

How shocking! Help me to carry one of these jugs home and I'll give you a large slice of bread.

*(*PINOCCHIO *eyes the jugs, but makes no answer.)*

With butter and jam.

*(*PINOCCHIO *is silent.)*

I will also give you a dish of ice cream—chocolate, strawberry, and vanilla.

(Disappointed at PINOCCHIO's *silent refusal, she picks up the two jugs to leave. Beginning to fear the loss of all the good things she has mentioned,* PINOCCHIO *decides to make the great physical effort which is so distasteful to him.)*

PINOCCHIO: All right!

(The BLUE FAIRY *gives* PINOCCHIO *one of the jugs. He staggers under the weight. The curtain falls.)*

SCENE TWO. *Inside the* BLUE FAIRY'S *house. The scene can be the same as in Act I, Scene 1. (As the curtain rises, the* BLUE FAIRY *and* PINOCCHIO *enter.* PINOCCHIO *is still carrying the jug and still groaning and mumbling discontentedly under his breath. The* BLUE FAIRY *helps him to put down the jug.* PINOCCHIO *heaves a great sigh and looks about hungrily. His eyes remain glued to two or three plates that are on the table. The* BLUE FAIRY, *much amused at the hint, places the chair near the table and invites* PINOCCHIO *to sit down.)*

BLUE FAIRY: Sit down, lad. Eat your bread and jam. All ready for you! *(Pause.)* No. I haven't forgotten the ice cream. That will come later.

(PINOCCHIO *sits down and falls to like a starving animal, not bothering about a fork or anything.)*

Don't you think you would feel lighter without your hat on?

(PINOCCHIO *snatches off his hat and throws it on the floor.)*

(The BLUE FAIRY *watches* PINOCCHIO *eat. When he has finished he wipes his mouth on his sleeve. The* BLUE FAIRY *throws off the shawl, disclosing her beautiful long braids of azure hair. His feast is finished to the crumb; he wipes his mouth with both cuffs and heaves a long, broken, devastating sigh.)*

BLUE FAIRY: Yes. It is too bad good things must come to an end. Did you like it, Pinocchio?

PINOCCHIO *(nods violently)*: Yes! Maybe. Could you . . .

(For the first time PINOCCHIO *raises his eyes to the* BLUE FAIRY, *and remains transfixed with his mouth open.)*

BLUE FAIRY: Well, well. Why all this sudden and wonderful surprise?

PINOCCHIO: You look like somebody I dream of—are you she? Yes, yes, yes! Your hair is just the same. Your eyes are the same. Your voice is the same. You have blue hair too, haven't you. You must be my dear Blue Fairy.

BLUE FAIRY: Am I? Let me see—perhaps I am she. How did you find me out? Who told you?

PINOCCHIO: It's because of my great big love for you: that's who told me. Oh, my Blue Fairy, my Blue Fairy! So it's you—really you?

BLUE FAIRY: Yes, Pinocchio. Are you really so glad to see me in real life.

PINOCCHIO: Yes, yes, yes, yes. Will you—can you be my mother because I want to have a mother like all the other boys, and grow tall. How do you grow tall?

BLUE FAIRY: That's my secret, Pinocchio—a deep secret.

PINOCCHIO: Teach it to me. Teach the secret to me because I would like to grow big.

BLUE FAIRY: But you can't grow, Pinocchio.

PINOCCHIO: And why can't I grow?

BLUE FAIRY: Because you haven't any roots. When you were a tree trunk it was different. But now you're all cut out and put together and you're a complete marionette with no roots anywhere—head or feet. Marionettes are born that way—they live that way—they never change.

PINOCCHIO: I'm tired of being like this—a marionette all made of wood. All the other boys always make fun of me and I have to kick them. It's time I was like the rest of them. I don't want to be me any more.

BLUE FAIRY: You could be a real boy too—

PINOCCHIO: I could?

BLUE FAIRY: If you deserved it.

PINOCCHIO: And what must I do to deserve it?

BLUE FAIRY: Something very, very simple and easy and all that.

PINOCCHIO: What?

BLUE FAIRY: Be good.

PINOCCHIO: Is that all? Ain't I?

BLUE FAIRY: No. You're everything to the contrary—everything but.

PINOCCHIO: But what?

BLUE FAIRY: Good. Boys who are good always obey. You, on the other hand . . .

PINOCCHIO: I never obey anybody.

BLUE FAIRY: Good boys like to study—like to work.

PINOCCHIO: And I like to play and be a tramp winter and summer.

BLUE FAIRY: Exactly. Good boys don't have to be dragged to school by their parents—they go joyfully.

PINOCCHIO: And as for me, school gives me a pain. But from today or tomorrow I intend to turn over a new leaf.

BLUE FAIRY: Will you promise me that?

PINOCCHIO: I promise it twice and three times! I want to become a real boy too, and I want to make my poor dada happy. Poor, poor dada! I wonder where he is right now?

BLUE FAIRY: I don't know, Pinocchio. I don't know.

PINOCCHIO: Will I ever be able to see him and hug him again?

BLUE FAIRY: Perhaps. Yes, I think so. In fact I'm quite sure of it.

PINOCCHIO: Hurray, hurray! Hurray for my Blue Fairy Mother. Now I will always be happy and I'll never be hungry. Is there any more ice cream?

BLUE FAIRY: Remember you must obey me in everything I say.

PINOCCHIO: Sure! Always!

BLUE FAIRY: Good. Beginning tomorrow you will start by going to school.

PINOCCHIO (receiving this news like a bucket of cold water): Oh!

BLUE FAIRY: Then later on when you know what studies you like best—you can begin to choose a profession or trade.

(PINOCCHIO *stares at the floor muttering. He has become very serious.*)

What are you muttering, Pinocchio? Speak so that I can hear you.

PINOCCHIO *(still not very loudly)*: I was just thinking that as far as school goes—I was thinking it's a little bit late for me to start to go to school.

BLUE FAIRY: Late? Well, did you ever! My dear little gentleman, it's never too late to learn.

PINOCCHIO: But it's not necessary to go to school or to learn a trade.

BLUE FAIRY: Oh, really? And why not?

PINOCCHIO: Oh, because! Because I'm too delicate to do any kind of work and books make me dizzy.

BLUE FAIRY: No. It's because you want to be lazy, shiftless, worthless, indolent, sluggish and overeat and oversleep until your brains—what specks you have—float away and stay there in dreamland. Am I right?

(PINOCCHIO *makes no answer. She takes him by the shoulders and shakes him until he rattles.*)

I don't mind bad boys. They are better than lazy, sleepy, gluttonous ones. You should have fallen into a bank, not a carpenter's shop. But I'm sure my Pinocchio didn't mean what he said—not this Pinocchio.

PINOCCHIO *(suddenly raising his eyes and promising like a general)*: I want to study. I want to work—go to school. I want to do everything you tell me, everything. I've been a wooden puppet long enough and I want to be a real boy even if I must go to school a very long time first. You promised to make me a real boy, didn't you?

BLUE FAIRY: I did and three cheers for my brave Pinocchio.

Now it's up to you—up to you. Pinocchio. Give me a kiss, darling, to celebrate your brave decision. Now, Pinocchio, you must show your brand-new mother that your resolution is a good one. You have still an hour before dinner. I'm going to leave you alone here with some books so that you can study and prepare yourself a little for school tomorrow. Now I am going to tell you a big secret. It is quite possible that you may be turned into a real boy within a week if you show real progress. Maybe it can be done tomorrow and we will celebrate it by having a very jolly party to which you can invite all your little friends. We will have ice cream and cocoa and other nice things. Now, Pinocchio, I say again that it is up to you.

PINOCCHIO: Hurray! Hurray! Hurray! I'm going to be a boy tomorrow. You'll see. I'll study very hard. But, Fairy Mother, wouldn't it be better if I started after dinner, because then I wouldn't be so hungry.

BLUE FAIRY: No. One studies much better before dinner. After dinner I want you to tell me all about what you've done. Then we'll spend the rest of the evening studying together, because you must have forgotten a great deal since your last day in school. You mustn't appear too stupid tomorrow.

PINOCCHIO: All right. What will there be for dinner?

BLUE FAIRY: Something that you will like very, very much. But for the present you must nail your mind to these. There!

(She places some books on the table and makes PINOCCHIO *sit by them.)*

Good-by until dinner time.

(The BLUE FAIRY *goes out and* PINOCCHIO *looks at the open pages of the books without enjoying them.)*

PINOCCHIO: Arithmetic. Geogafry. Gramma.

(This seems to be the lesser of the evils. He reads slowly and brokenly.)

The—fox—and—the—grapes. A hun—gry—fox—a—hungry—fox—was walking—one—day—in—the—forest —Soon—he—came—to—a—place—where—he—saw—grapes—hang—ing—from—a—high—vine—He—licked—his—chops—and—said—Those—grapes—will—make—a —fine—dinner.

(Someone is heard whistling a half melancholy, half gay tune outside. PINOCCHIO *pricks up his ears and listens. The whistling continues.* PINOCCHIO *tries to read, but finds it difficult to concentrate with the music outside. The whistling turns into a song.)*

VOICE: Midnight is the time of day
When boys and girls should come and play.
The coach is coming, one, two, three.
And up to ten for you and me.

PINOCCHIO: Gee! Who can that be?

(He rushes to the window and peers out, making every effort to locate the voice.)

Hello, you out there. Who are you?

VOICE: I am Wick. Everybody calls me Dry Wick. Who are you?

PINOCCHIO: I'm Pinocchio. I'm starting school tomorrow.

WICK: Hello, Pinocchio!

(He appears on the other side of the window, dressed as any lazy youngster would be.)

What are you doing in this funny house?

PINOCCHIO: I live here. It's not a funny house. It's a nice house. It's my mother's house.

WICK: Oh, that's different.

PINOCCHIO: I'm glad to see you, Wicky.

WICK: Yeah.

PINOCCHIO: Come on in. You can climb in. But don't make any noise, because I'm supposed to be studying.

WICK: Naw. I haven't got time. I'm in a hurry.

(He lounges as if he had all the time in the world.)

PINOCCHIO: Oh, yeah? Where are you going?

WICK: Oh, some place.

PINOCCHIO: Gee. I wish I was going too.

WICK: Come on along, then.

PINOCCHIO: I can't. I promised my mother I would study. And next week, or maybe tomorrow, I am going to be a real boy—not wood any more. And I'm going to have a great big party where all my friends will come and get ice cream and cocoa and then wish me good luck. You want to come to my party—maybe tomorrow?

WICK: Naw. I can't.

PINOCCHIO: Don't you like ice cream and cocoa?

WICK: Not much. I got something else to do. Good-by, Pinocchio.

PINOCCHIO: What's your hurry, Wick? Where you going? Can't you tell?

WICK: I've got to go and wait for midnight—twelve o'clock.

PINOCCHIO: What for?

WICK: I'm leaving.

PINOCCHIO: Where are you going?

WICK: Way—far—far-away.

PINOCCHIO: Really? What for?

WICK: Because. I'm going to live there. I don't like this place. Too many schools—teachers—mothers and fathers—everything. I'm going to the best country in the world—and never come back.

PINOCCHIO: Gosh! What is it called?

WICK: What is it called? Merry-Go-Round Land. Why don't you come along too?

PINOCCHIO: Nope. I can't.

WICK: Can't. Why can't you?

PINOCCHIO: I made a promise. That's why I can't.

WICK: Promise? Believe me, you'll be sorry. Where can you find a place like that here for us kids? No schools, no teachers, and no books. In that swell Merry-Go-Round Land nobody ever needs to study. There's no school on Saturday and every week has six Saturdays and one Sunday. The summer vacation begins on the first of June and ends the thirty-first of next May. That's what I call a country—a civilized country.

PINOCCHIO: And what do people do there all day long?

WICK: Do? Everything. Anything. They eat, play, yawn, stretch, and then go to sleep. Next morning they begin all over again.

PINOCCHIO: Um. It sounds pretty good.

WICK: Well, make up your mind, if you want to come along —otherwise good-by. I don't want to be late.

PINOCCHIO: How do you go there?

WICK: By coach. A beautiful coach passes around at midnight and those who have sense get on board.

PINOCCHIO: But you've got lots of time.

WICK: Yeah. But I like to be early—get a good seat.

PINOCCHIO: Gee, I wish it were midnight. I would like to see what the coach is like.

WICK: Come along.

PINOCCHIO: But I can't.

WICK: Maybe you could see it now, 'way in the distance. It goes all over the mountains and you see the bright lamps all lit and shining.

PINOCCHIO: Gosh. Maybe I could come and get back before my mother ever knows it.

WICK: Of course you could if you want to. Of course, if you

don't want to, I'll have to say good-by, because I can't wait much longer.

PINOCCHIO: No kidding, Wick, are you absolutely sure that there are no schools at all in that country?

WICK: Absolutely. I got evidence. There's not even a school's shadow. Nothing.

PINOCCHIO: No teachers?

WICK: Not one.

PINOCCHIO: No truant officers?

WICK: Of course not.

PINOCCHIO: And you're never forced to study?

WICK: Never, never, never. Just play, sleep, eat and all that.

PINOCCHIO: Some country! That's a swell place. I've never been there, but I can figure it out.

WICK: Nothing like it. Well, are you coming?

PINOCCHIO: No use. I've got to stay here and suffer. I promised my mother, the Blue Fairy, I would. And she promised I'd become a real boy and I should keep my promise.

WICK: That's all right with me. Good-by, Pinocchio. Regards to Mr. Rithmetic, Gramma, Geofagy and Spelling—and the principal if you meet him in the street.

(As he says his last sentence, DRY WICK retires slowly out of sight. PINOCCHIO follows him with his eyes.)

PINOCCHIO: Good-by, Wick. Have a pleasant journey and when you have nothing else to do think of me once in a while.

(He turns his back resolutely on the tempting figure. But DRY WICK's song torments him again, so he leans out of the window with great longing.)

WICK'S VOICE: Midnight is the time of day
　　　　　　When boys and girls should come and play.
　　　　　　The coach is coming, one, two, three,
　　　　　　And up to ten for you and me.

PINOCCHIO: Hey, Wick! Wicky!

WICK'S VOICE: What?

PINOCCHIO: Come here just a minute.

WICK'S VOICE: I can't. Getting late.

PINOCCHIO: Only a minute! Are you absolutely positively sure that every day is Saturday except Sunday!

WICK'S VOICE: Absolutely. Positively.

PINOCCHIO: Cross your heart? Gosh, what a place! And vaca, tions start the first of June and end the last of next May. Are you sure?

WICK'S VOICE: Come on and I'll prove it to you.

PINOCCHIO: Gee! I would just like to see it. Good-by, Wick. Have a pleasant journey.

(He paces the floor, examines the books, which make him feel extremely sick. He rushes to the window.)

Wicky!

WICK'S VOICE: Yes?

PINOCCHIO: Wait. I'm coming. But I'll just take a look at the coach.

(He tiptoes to the door and listens. He then lays the books all open on the table, puts on his hat, and climbs out of the window to join WICK.*)*

I'll study when I come back.

(The curtain falls as WICK *sings his song again.)*

Midnight is the time of day,

When boys and girls should come and play.

The coach is coming, one, two, three.

And up to ten for you and me.

SCENE THREE. *This scene represents a highway in the woods. A few trees are scattered about. To one side there is a wooden bench. In the ground is planted a large signboard which reads "Coach Station for Merry-Go-Round Land."* PINOCCHIO *and*

DRY WICK *are seated on the bench when the curtain rises.*

PINOCCHIO: I wonder what time it is.

WICK: I don't know. But it must be getting late. We ought to see the coach any minute now. Funny, it's not in sight yet. Must have got delayed somewhere.

PINOCCHIO: Maybe it's not coming.

WICK: No chance. It comes around just like the roosters have to crow in the morning.

PINOCCHIO: I wish it would hurry up, because I'd like to see it at least.

WICK: We ought to see it any minute. I wonder what's the matter.

(They sit silently for a few moments. PINOCCHIO *then rises and peers hard in the distance without detecting anything.)*

PINOCCHIO: I guess I'll go, Wick. It's not going to come.

WICK: Stay a while and you'll see it.

PINOCCHIO: No, no. I ought to go home.

WICK: Aw. Wait two minutes more.

PINOCCHIO: I've stayed out too long already. The Blue Fairy will get worried.

WICK: What's the matter? Is she afraid that the sparrows will eat you up? Who could eat you up? Not even an alligator.

PINOCCHIO: All right. I'll wait only two more minutes.

(There is another short silence, during which PINOCCHIO *is day-dreaming over the advantages of the blessed country* WICK *is going to.)*

No schools at all? Are you sure?

WICK: None at all. Nobody even talks about them.

PINOCCHIO *(looking once more in the distance)*: Nothing yet. Well, good-by, Wick. Hope you have a nice ride.

WICK: It's not two minutes yet. What a mama's pet!

PINOCCHIO: It must be more than two minutes. I'll get scolded.

WICK: What do you care? That's all mothers are good for anyway. They've got to scold to be happy.

PINOCCHIO: Will you be alone in the coach or what?

WICK: Alone? There will be more than a hundred other kids.

PINOCCHIO: And how much do they charge?

WICK: Charge? Ha, ha, ha! It's all free. What do you think?

PINOCCHIO: Gee! Free! You're lucky.

WICK: I know it.

(A sweet-sounding trumpet is heard blowing in the distance. WICK jumps to his feet. They both look eagerly in the direction from whence it comes.)

That's it! It's coming! See the lights? It's coming very fast. It must be late.

(A jingling of bells now begins to be heard. PINOCCHIO stares with open mouth, unable to say a word.)

Well, good-by, Pinocchio. Now that you've seen the coach and don't think I was lying, you can go home.

PINOCCHIO: I'm late anyway. Half an hour more won't matter. I think I'll wait till you get in.

WICK: How about your Fairy Mother? Won't she worry?

PINOCCHIO: Let her. When she gets tired of worrying she'll go to sleep.

WICK: It's up to you.

(The bells and trumpet get louder and louder.)

PINOCCHIO: And you mean that you'll never have to study any more?

WICK: Never, never, never!

PINOCCHIO: What luck!

(The coach makes its entrance. It is drawn by as many donkeys as it is convenient to use on the scene, any number from two to twenty. The harnesses are trimmed with little brass bells, which tinkle in gay confusion when in movement. The coach may be of any design on four wheels, with benches

for the children to sit on. In front is the COACHMAN'S *seat, where the driver sits cracking his whip. The* COACHMAN *is a short but very round little man and should look like a ball of butter, more than anything else. He is soft and unctuous, and when he speaks, his voice resembles the purring of a cat that wants to be in the good graces of his mistress. His small fat mouth wears a perpetual smile. His costume in general is like any coachman's, with extra shiny brass buttons. In the coach are as many puppets as can be seated uncomfortably. They are packed in and all are shouting with joy. The lighting should be such as to suggest night, so that the lamps on the coach can shine in their brightness.)*

COACHMAN: Whoa! Whoa! Very merry, nimble, jingly ones. Whoa! *(The coach stops.)* All aboard! Good evening, little gentlemen. Good evening, my darlings. Do you also wish to join us in our rollicking, frolicking ride to Merry-Go-Round Land? That's the place for little gentlemen, little gentlemen of leisure. That's the place—that's the place— where you won't have to wash your hands or face. Are you coming along with us, little gentlemen?

WICK: Yes, Mr. Coachman. I want to come.

COACHMAN: Wise boy, wise boy. And lucky too. Oh yes, yes. Lucky! But I warn you—it grieves me to tell you, little darling, that there is no more room in the coach. See for yourself. It's all full. Every seat taken twice.

(The boys in the coach, who are laughing and singing, invite WICK *to join them in spite of their cramped quarters.)*

WICK: Oh, that's nothing, Mr. Coachman. I don't need to get inside. I can sit on the edge in the back.

COACHMAN: What a splendid little hero! Splendid! *(To* PINOCCHIO*)* And what about you? Do you intend to stay behind? Surely you must come with us too. How can you resist such a gloriously rollicking trip? All aboard the heavenly ship before I crack my whip! My little puppet, are you coming or are you staying?

PINOCCHIO: I'm staying, I think. Thanks just the same. I'm going back home to study and go to school and . . . all that.

COACHMAN: Oh, he is going to desert us. Poor us! We shall miss you. You're such a desirable specimen. He likes school better, better than the land where freedom is one hundred and one per cent. Oh dear, no cheer, come tear, come here, come here.

ALL THE BOYS *(in disappointment)*: A—a—a—a—ah!

WICK: Come along, Pinocchio!

ALL THE BOYS: Come on, Pinocchio.

PINOCCHIO: No, no, no, no! *(His refusal is rather weak.)*

COACHMAN: Pinocchio! Are you Pinocchio? Well, well, this is the famous Pinocchio? The darling Pinocchio? At last I have met you. Come, Pinocchio, you must come along to our country, our beloved Merry-Go-Round Land. It will not be complete until you come too.

ALL THE BOYS: Come on, Pinocchio!

PINOCCHIO: But if I come along, what will my good Fairy Mother say?

COACHMAN: My poor dear deluded Pinocchio. Over there we don't worry about such things. Do we, darlings?

ALL THE BOYS: No!

WICK: Aw, come on, Pinocchio. You know you want to come. You make me sick with your mama's boy stuff.

COACHMAN: We all beg you, Pinocchio—gallant Pinocchio, come along with us—don't we?

ALL THE BOYS: Come along with us, Pinocchio!

COACHMAN: Sh! Let him make his own decision. Take a moment to think, Pinocchio, and don't throw the moment away, Pinocchio—the golden moment.

(There is silence for a few seconds, during which PINOC-
CHIO *reflects very hard. He sighs once, twice, three times.
Then comes the decision.)*

PINOCCHIO: Make a little room for me. I want to come too.

ALL THE BOYS: Hurray!

COACHMAN: Brave, gallant, darling! Wise Pinocchio! I knew
you would. There isn't room for another sardine inside
the coach, my love; but to show how much I esteem you I
will give up my own place to you, up here.

PINOCCHIO: And what will you do?

COACHMAN: Oh, never mind me. I can walk, my little ones, I
can walk.

PINOCCHIO: No. Thank you very much, Mr. Coachman. I
won't permit you to do that for me. I would much rather
ride horseback on one of these mules.

(He approaches the nearest mule and mounts it. The
COACHMAN *climbs on his box and the coach is ready to continue on its joyous useless journey.)*

Are we all here, my darlings? All safely on board?

ALL THE BOYS: Yes, yes!

COACHMAN: Then we are ready to move on. Giddap, giddap,
my merry, nimble, jingly ones. Giddap, giddap!

*(The boys hurrah and shout, the bells jingle, the whip
cracks and the coach begins to move on. At this point the
stage lights should all go out, leaving the scene dimly lit by
coach lamps. The donkeys can be heard galloping with their
bells jingling and the whip cracking over them. But in reality
the coach remains in the same spot so that the following
scene can take place. The* DONKEY *on which* PINOCCHIO *is
riding is heard braying as though it were weeping in a voice
that is half human.)*

DONKEY: He—ee—haw! Poor Pinocchio, poor Pinocchio.
You'll be sorry. Hee—ee—ee! You'll be sorry.

PINOCCHIO (*very much frightened*): Who's that? Who's there?

SOME OF THE BOYS: What, Pinocchio? What's the matter?

COACHMAN: Whoa—a—aa—aa.

(*The donkeys stop galloping.*)

What is it, my precious ones?

SOME OF THE BOYS: Pinocchio is scared. He hollered!

COACHMAN: Scared, Pinocchio? What! The brave, gallant, heroic Pinocchio scared? No, not he. What are you afraid of, Pinocchio? Nothing to be afraid of.

PINOCCHIO: I'm not afraid. I thought I—that—I just said: "Who's there?"

COACHMAN: Is that all? There's nobody here but us, Pinocchio. Nobody but gay, galloping, frolicking us. Come—three good, loud cheers for us.

ALL THE BOYS: Hurrah, hurrah, hurrah!

COACHMAN: Giddap, giddap, giddap!

(*The donkeys resume their galloping. He quietly sings the following song as they gallop along.*)

They sleep, sleep, rock and sleep
All night as the well is deep.
I wake, wake, all night I wake,
And while they sleep I harvest make.

(*The voice of the same* DONKEY *is heard again above the rollicking.*)

DONKEY: Hee—ee—ee—aw! You're certainly tough wood, Pinocchio. Better for you if you had nailed some books on your head. Where do you think you're going? Wait—you'll see. Look at me. Only donkeys want to go to Merry-Go-Round Land. You'll find out. You'll be sorry and weep too—when it's too late.

PINOCCHIO (*Almost frantic with fear, he jumps off the* DONKEY *and screams for the* COACHMAN *to stop.*): Stop! Stop! Stop!

COACHMAN: Who—o—o—o—o—a. Who is it? What is it?

Have any of my precious bundles of treasure fallen off? Or are there robbers attacking? Don't be afraid of robbers.

PINOCCHIO (*holding the head of the weeping* DONKEY): Look, Mr. Coachman, what's the matter with this donkey?

SOME OF THE BOYS: Bring a lantern.

(*The* COACHMAN *approaches with a lantern.*)

PINOCCHIO: He is crying. This poor donkey is crying.

SOME OF THE BOYS: Crying? Let me see! I never saw a donkey cry before.

(*Some of the boys get out of the coach and examine the weeping* DONKEY.)

ALL THE BOYS: A—a—a—a—ah—oh!

COACHMAN: Well, well, weeping again. He has the disease. The only cure for that disease is to pay no attention to it.

PINOCCHIO: I think I heard him speak. Have you taught him to speak too?

COACHMAN: He learned it by himself—just a few words—to pass the time while he gallops.

PINOCCHIO: Poor thing!

(*The other boys take up* PINOCCHIO's *refrain and repeat:* "Poor thing—poor thing!")

COACHMAN (*once more on his box seat*): Come now, my little jewels packed in this precious little rolling treasure box— no more delay. Let the dear little donkey have his little weep. All aboard and hold tight. Mount, Pinocchio. Let us not waste the fresh, dark, delightful night. We still have a long, long, long way to ride. Giddap, giddap! My strong little precious gallopers! Giddap, giddap! Take all the reins! Full speed! Giddap, giddap!

(*The galloping and jingling and shouting are resumed with increased vigor and the curtain falls as the coach drives off the scene.*)

SCENE FOUR. *The curtain rises and discloses Merry-Go-Round Land. In fact one can hear the pandemonium through the curtain before it rises. There are many gayly painted little houses clustered together. The effect is somewhat similar to that presented by the dozens of side-show booths in a circus. Wherever there is wall space it is decorated with inscriptions such as "Down with Skule," "Long Live Marbles and Tops," "Down with Arithmitik!" "Tree Cheers for Merry-Go-Round." Merry-Go-Round Land as pictured in this scene should give the impression of a toy city come to life and it may be as modern as one pleases. The little houses may be built one on top of the other and away off at all impossible angles, defying both gravity and geometry. The whole idea, of course, is rebellion against anything taught in the schools. There isn't a sign of a schoolhouse, church, or flag to be seen anywhere. The place is alive with boy puppets engaged in a thousand pranks and games. Some play leapfrog, some roll hoops, others play blindman's buff, some sing, some dance, some blow horns, some run about and tumble in clown costumes. Nearly all of them wear something fantastic such as improvised paper hats, wooden swords, and cardboard shields and helmets. Some ride hobby horses and others tricycles. There is whistling, clapping, yelling, laughing but no weeping. In the middle of the street there is a boy impersonating ɩ traffic cop. He has taken it upon himself to regulate the traffic of toy automobiles, bicycles and fire engines, which scoot by at high speed. One of the vehicles runs into him unawares and carries him off in a most undignified manner.* PINOCCHIO *and* WICK, *who have been occupied with one thing or another from the beginning of the scene, now engage in conversation.*

PINOCCHIO: Gee, Wick, what a place, what a life! This is the life.

WICK: See? You wouldn't believe me, would you? And you didn't want to come. I knew what I was talking about.

PINOCCHIO: I know it.

WICK: You would have been out of luck. School—lessons— and obey-your-Fairy-Mother bunk! If you don't have to worry about those things it's because you took my advice. I told you how it would be. Was I right or not?

PINOCCHIO: You were right and I'll always believe you from now on. I'll bet a million dollars that this is the best and happiest city in the whole world—the whole world, mind you!

WICK: Easy! I wouldn't bet you because I'd lose.

PINOCCHIO: We've been here pretty long now. How long is it?

WICK: I think it's about five months.

PINOCCHIO: It's so nice. It is almost too good. Sometimes I wish I had something to worry about.

WICK: I don't. This life suits me and I don't want any change anyhow.

PINOCCHIO: Oh, me too, I was only meaning how swell it was.

(WICK *walks off whistling.* PINOCCHIO *suddenly claps his hands to his ears and rushes into his house. Quickly tack donkey's ears on* PINOCCHIO'S *head. He peeks out into the street fearfully—afraid to let anyone see these sudden, disgraceful appendages. Finally observing that the coast is clear, he comes out of his house and examines these strange ears of his more carefully in the daylight. They are so long that he can pull them around and look at them, which he does in great alarm. He feels them, he tries to pull them off, hoping they were put there by a mischievous companion. But pulling them only brings pain. At first he is furious; he stamps his feet angrily, muttering disparaging remarks. Then, his rage spent, he becomes disconsolate and begins to weep. He weeps and wails and beats his head against the wall and wrings his*

hands until the noise attracts the attention of a DORMOUSE
who lives in the little house next to PINOCCHIO. *Dress the*
DORMOUSE *in a tight-fitting costume of flannel and give her*
a bushy tail. She may also wear a little nurse's cap and apron.
In fact, we may even take the liberty to stick a red cross on
her apron.)

DORMOUSE *(sticking her head through the window)*: My, my,
my! What is the trouble, little neighbor? You seem to be
in a terrible plight. Can I help you?

PINOCCHIO: I'm sick—very, very sick. *(Weeps bitterly.)* I've
got a terrible disease and I'm afraid.

DORMOUSE: Sick? Oh, then I can help you. *(She comes out*
of the house.) What hurts you? Give me your pulse.

(*She feels* PINOCCHIO's *pulse, puts her ear to his stomach,*
examines his feet, taps his chest and finally his head. It is then
that she really discovers the ears and becomes very much con-
cerned about them. She examines them closely, shaking her
head and sighing.)

My dear little friend, I have some bad news for you;
bad news.

PINOCCHIO *(bawls loudly)*: What bad news?

DORMOUSE: I'm afraid to tell you.

PINOCCHIO *(bawling)*: W—a-aa-aa—a! Hurry up and tell me.

DORMOUSE: You have a very peculiar kind of fever, but very
serious—very, very serious. A terrible fever!

PINOCCHIO: W—a—a—a—a! What kind of a fever?

DORMOUSE: It is what we call Donkeyitis.

PINOCCHIO: What does that mean? I don't know what that
means.

DORMOUSE: Well, Pinocchio, I will have to explain it to you.
Sooner or later you will have to know. *(She examines the*
ears again.) I'm afraid it will be sooner—much sooner. Yes,
in about an hour or even less this fever will change you

from—whatever you are, no matter what you are, boy, puppet or anything else—into something entirely different.

PINOCCHIO: What?

DORMOUSE *(examining the ears once more)*: In your case, you will be changed into a nice, healthy, prancing, stubborn donkey.

PINOCCHIO: Wa—a—a—a—a! A what?

DORMOUSE: Donkey. You've seen them. The little donkeys that drive little wagons to the market. You know the little carts piled up with cabbages, lettuce, and tomatoes. But I think you'll be more handsome.

PINOCCHIO: W—a—a—a—a! Poor Pinocchio! Poor me!

(He stamps about and pulls at his long ears, which only result in making him scream the louder.)

DORMOUSE: Pinocchio! Pinocchio! Aren't you ashamed? Be a little hero. Haven't you had a good time here? Has anybody bothered you or made you do disagreeable things? You chose your own way, didn't you? You've played your fill, you've eaten your fill of the choicest things, and you've overslept. Here's the result. You've got to pay something for it. There's no help for it. Take it philosophically. Destiny is destiny. You might be changed into something worse—not much, but something.

PINOCCHIO: Am I really going to be a donkey?

DORMOUSE: Absolutely; but not for a whole hour or so, anyway.

PINOCCHIO: But it's not my fault. It's Wick's fault.

DORMOUSE: Who's Wick?

PINOCCHIO: My best friend. But he's not my best friend. I only thought so. He's not even my worst friend. I wanted to go home and go to school, and he said: Don't do that. Come with me to a place where nobody learns lessons. Everybody plays all the time. Wa—a—a—a!

DORMOUSE: And why did you take his advice?

PINOCCHIO: Because my head is all wood, and I guess I must be solid. Oh, my dear Blue Fairy Mother, I'm going to be a donkey. Poor me! Poor Pinocchio! And now I'll never be a real boy. Just a donkey. Poor me! Poor Pinocchio! I don't want to be a donkey.

(He pulls at his ears again and screams and stamps and carries on like a bad, spoiled INSIGNIFICANT that he is. The DORMOUSE *quietly watches and shakes her head. In the middle of* PINOCCHIO'S *frantic despair the gay sound of drum and cymbals is heard. A moment later the fat* COOK *makes his appearance beating cymbals. He is all dressed up in fancy colored tissue and crepe paper so that he looks like a fantastic herald of a large birthday cake. At the sound of the cymbals all the boys rush back on the scene and begin to crowd around the* COOK.)

DORMOUSE: Let us go inside, Pinocchio, where we can hear ourselves.

(They enter PINOCCHIO'S *house.)*

COOK *(making a noise similar to a hen calling her little chicks)*: Coot—coot—coot—coot—coot! Little ones, starving ones, tiny ones, shiny ones, hungry ones, one and all— coot, coot, coot, coot! Come along, come along, come along, run along, scoot along, and bring your little mouths, big mouths, hungry mouths, open mouths, along. Come catch the delicious, exquisite morsels off my dishes. Come catch the dumplings, tarts, pies, pastries, candied fruits, gingerbread, raisin bread, sweetbreads, cream cheese, head cheese, pungent cheese, pickles, frankfurters, with sweet and hot mustard, ginger ale, soda pop, ice cream sodas, any flavor, sundaes, and when you finish, stay and start all over again! Coot, coot, coot, coot, coot, coot, coot, coot, coot!

(As he recites his tempting menu of the day he punctu-

ates the items with his cymbals and performs what may roughly be called a dance. The boys rush in from every direction and dance and chatter about him like so many real chicks impatient to be fed. As the Cook *goes off scattering sweet culinary phrases about him, the crowd of boys follow him like the rats that followed the Pied Piper. The scene is completely deserted. Knowing this,* Pinocchio *emerges from his house again, this time wearing a very tall cylindrical cardboard hat which completely hides his ears from the public. He goes to* Wick's *house and knocks on the door. At first there is no answer, but finally, after repeated loud knocking and calling,* Wick's *timid voice comes through the door.)*

Wick's Voice: Who is it?

Pinocchio: It's me. Pinocchio. Come out here, Wick.

Wick's Voice: What do you want?

Pinocchio: I want to tell you something. Don't you feel hungry?

Wick's Voice: No.

Pinocchio: Well, come out anyway.

Wick's Voice: Wait a couple of minutes.

(Pinocchio *waits a little while impatiently. He walks to and fro in front of the door restlessly. He tries to peep through the key hole. He knocks again, walks some more, mutters to himself, but* Wick *still delays.)*

Pinocchio: What's the matter, Wick? Hurry up!

Wick's Voice: Can't you wait a minute?

(Pinocchio *waits another long minute. Unable to stand it any longer he kicks the door very hard. At the same moment* Wick *opens it and comes out cautiously.* Pinocchio's *amazement is very great indeed when he lays eyes on* Wick, *for he too is wearing a tall cylindrical cardboard hat exactly the same as* Pinocchio's. Wick's *surprise is no less great when he sees* Pinocchio's *headgear. The two boys stand and gape at each other, unable to say a word for a few seconds. When they get over their first shock they are both seized with a desire to laugh, which they suppress.)*

PINOCCHIO: I just wanted to ask you how you feel, Wick.

WICK: I feel fine; as rich as a mouse in a house made of cheese.

PINOCCHIO: Do you really mean it?

WICK: Sure. Don't you believe me?

PINOCCHIO: Uh huh. And what do you wear that big stovepipe for on top of your head?

WICK: That? The doctor made me put it on because I fell and hurt my knee. What about you, Pinocchio? Why are you hiding in that tunnel up to your nose?

PINOCCHIO: I stubbed my toe too. So the doctor gave me that bandage.

WICK: That's tough on you, Pinocchio.

PINOCCHIO: Yeah. Tough on you too, Wick.

WICK: Yeah. *(There is a short silence during which the two boys scrutinize each other.)*

PINOCCHIO: Say, Wick, were your ears ever sick?

WICK: Naw. Never. Were yours?

PINOCCHIO: Nope. But since this morning I felt a pain in this ear.

WICK: Yeah? That's funny. Me too. In this ear.

PINOCCHIO: You too? Which ear is it?

WICK: Both. How about you?

PINOCCHIO: Both too. Maybe we have the same disease.

WICK: I wouldn't be surprised.

PINOCCHIO: Want to do me a favor, Wick?

WICK: Sure. What?

PINOCCHIO: Let me take a look at your ears.

WICK: Why not? But first let me see yours, Pinocchio.

PINOCCHIO: I asked you first.

WICK: No siree. You show me your ears first.

PINOCCHIO: All right. Let's make a bargain. You turn your back and I'll turn mine. We'll count three and then turn around with our hats off. Are you willing?

WICK: O. K.

PINOCCHIO: Get ready.

(They turn back to back and take off their cardboard camouflages. They count—one, two, three—throw the cardboard hats flying and face about. At the sight of each other's ears they shriek with laughter, point to the monstrous hairy visitations. They laugh and laugh and suddenly WICK is taken with some violent cramps which make him writhe and dance about.)

WICK: Help me, Pinocchio! Help! Help!

PINOCCHIO: What's the matter, Wick? Stand up. Why don't you stand up?

WICK: Wow! I can't stand on my feet!

(WICK continues to dance around and yell for help. He finally gets down on all fours and gallops about as if he were a donkey. He goes around in a circle while PINOCCHIO remains petrified in the center. Finally WICK gallops off the scene still lamenting. Behind the scene substitute a donkey puppet quickly as possible. Left alone, PINOCCHIO remains bewildered and frightened for some moments. Then in a flash he, too, is seized with the same kind of a fit. He leaps and dances and screams, and finally falls on all fours to gallop about just as WICK has done. PINOCCHIO also gallops off the scene. This action should be timed so that PINOCCHIO remains on the scene until WICK makes his return as a donkey. PINOCCHIO then gallops off and he returns as a donkey. The two donkeys frolic about wildly, and their efforts to talk only result in loud hysterical braying. The noise of the donkeys reaches the ears of the boss, who is none other than the fat, soft, unctuous COACHMAN. He appears on the scene dressed exactly as before.

He is accompanied by BILLY *who is dressed in the conventional ringmaster outfit: high hat, cutaway coat, white trousers, boots and whip.)*

COACHMAN: Ha, ha. I thought I recognized my little darlings; particularly my special extra pretty precious here. Look at him, Mr. Billy. That feathery prancer there. Did you ever see such talent before? Hoopee, my love, show your genius to this elegant gentleman here. Come, my precious pin-legged Pinocchio.

(He prods and strikes PINOCCHIO *to make him prance higher. The circus master looks* PINOCCHIO *over with all his expert professional manner: but says nothing. He pokes* PINOCCHIO *with the handle of his whip.)*

MR. BILLY: Not bad. Solid. I think I can do something with him. Not bad. Possibilities. Might be even trained as a circus star. How much?

COACHMAN: Take him, Mr. Billy. We won't quarrel about price. Did we ever quarrel about price? We never quarrel about price. You want him, Mr. Billy. I want you to have him. Best bargain that you have ever had. His name is Pinocchio.

MR. BILLY: Pinocchio. How about the other?

COACHMAN: Not so good for your purpose, Mr. Billy. A little on the dull side, heavy, lazy. In your circus you want something with metal. Bright, brittle, clear, sparkling metal— like jewels. Pinocchio, yes. This one, no. Good business is straight business.

MR. BILLY *(whacks* WICK *with his whip, making him bray mournfully)*: I need a donkey or two just to carry some heavy loads. I'll take that too if it's cheap.

COACHMAN: Take him for a song, Mr. Billy. We won't argue about this one at all. Come, my new-born babies. You are going to join Mr. Billy's circus.

(He ties ropes around their necks and starts to lead them out. Both the poor donkeys resist and bray loudly in despair, but it does them no good.)

What? You object to going to the circus? Mr. Billy's circus? The biggest, grandest, funniest and proudest spectacle in the world? The impudence of my little darlings! Come along, precious ones! You won't feel that way after you've seen it. Come along, come along, come along.

(The COACHMAN *leads the two donkeys out by force.* MR. BILLY *follows behind and helps along by letting the beasts have some elegantly placed strokes of his whip on their hind quarters. The curtain falls.)*

ACT III

SCENE ONE. *Both the first and second scenes occur on the sawdust circular floor of a one-ring circus. Only half of the ring is visible to the audience. The other half is imagined on the audience side of the curtain. The back is a semi-circular barrier, behind which are the benches which later will be occupied by the spectators. The background is a plain drop.*

For the first scene there are two temporary stalls on the semi-circular floor, one at either end, which are used for housing the performing animals. One is empty and one is occupied by a young zebra. The stage lights should be concentrated on the two stalls with very little or no light on the rest of the scene. The costume of the zebra can be made of a black and white striped material. Bright circus colors must be in evidence. Borders of red, yellow and blue decorate the various properties. Sawdust on the floor will add to the effect. When the curtain rises the groom is polishing a brass harness, which may be made of oilcloth, decorated with brass rings. He is dressed in white cotton trousers, a red flannel shirt and black boots.

TONY *(to the zebra)*: How's my little peppermint stick this evening? *(The zebra neighs.)* That's good. *(The zebra neighs.)* Oh, she's hungry, is she? *(The zebra neighs.)* Well, we can fix that. Let us stop up the big hole in little Peppy's tummy.

(He gives PEPPERMINT *a handful of hay, singing as he does so.)*

Oh, the circus sure can work us
And it looks like fun and play,
All night long we move along
And perform the whole long day.
(The zebra neighs loudly.)

What are you yelling about, Peppy? You're not in the real working class yet—not yet, but you will be.

*(*BILLY, *the circus master, enters, prodding* PINOCCHIO *along with his whip.)*

BILLY: Here, Tony, here's another one.

TONY: Well, I'll be . . . What is it?

BILLY: It's a—well, it's Pinocchio. That's his name. An ordinary young mule—a little stiff here and there but you can take that out of him. Think he'll ever amount to anything?

TONY *(examining the forlorn* PINOCCHIO *very carefully)*: Why not? If his brains are as good as his name he ought to be a circus sensation. "Pinocchio!" Imagine that on a poster.

BILLY: Just what I thought. Glad you feel the same way.

(He slaps PINOCCHIO *on the haunch with the butt end of his whip.)*

I think we can make him learn. We may have to break two or three dozen whips—but what of that?

TONY: He looks good to me. We going to be friends, Pinocchio?

(He slaps PINOCCHIO *on the neck, the back, etc.* PINOC-
CHIO *is frightened and brays.)*

Now, now, donkey, don't be afraid of me. I'm the one
that feeds you.

BILLY: That's right, Pinocchio. That's Mr. Feed-Bag. So
get to know him and love him. Feed him and put him to
bed, Tony. We'll start him on his routine in the morning.

(He exits, leaving PINOCCHIO *in* TONY's *hands.* TONY
*takes a brush and begins to groom and comb his coat until
it shines.)*

TONY: My, my, my! You poor, neglected Pinocchio, I don't
believe you've ever been combed or brushed. Have you?
Tony will show you how nice you can look! Bright as a
mirror! With that thick coat of yours you ought to shine
brighter than a mirror. Now, now, Pinocchio, whoa! That
doesn't hurt. No faking. Not with me, little fellow. I've
known your father, your father's father and your father's
father's father's father—and some of them were much wiser
than you. Whoa! Git, my precious!

(He turns PINOCCHIO *this way and that to admire his slick
coat.)*

A bath like this once a day and you will glisten like the
gem of the opera.

*(*TONY *leads him into the empty stall and places a box
of hay before him.* PINOCCHIO *takes up a mouthful and spits
it out again with a mournful bray.)*

What? You don't like hay? Never mind. A matter of
bringing up.

(He puts a bag of oats before PINOCCHIO, *who treats it
the same way.)*

What? Oats neither? Excuse me, Excellency. I've insulted
Prince Pinocchio. You were born under a comical star. If
you haven't eaten this up in two weeks, I'll see that the

cook of his majesty Brass Buttons serves you with some very choice chickens out of the royal barnyard. Good night, Pinocchio, good night. Good night, Peppy. Talk to your new neighbor. He'll need some of your philosophy.

(He exits. All is quiet for a little while, then PINOCCHIO *begins to moan softly. The young zebra, who has observed everything, now begins to laugh. She goes over to* PINOCCHIO's *stall and eats some of the oats that* PINOCCHIO *spurns.)*

ZEBRA: Oats! Um, um! What's wrong with these oats? You don't know how lucky you are. I never get this much oats.

PINOCCHIO: Wa—a—a—a! I'm hungry!

ZEBRA: Better eat some then, because if you don't intend to I do! Um! Try it.

*(*PINOCCHIO *eats some of the oats, and much to his surprise, it doesn't taste badly. He keeps his nose in the bag so that the zebra cannot get at it again.)*

So you like it, hey? Don't choke over it.

(She begins to eat some of PINOCCHIO's *hay.* PINOCCHIO *finishes the oats, and then, still very hungry, he helps the zebra finish the hay.)*

Say, Pinocchio, you don't like hay, do you? Mama! I think you would eat pebbles. You're a pretty good actor, you are! You ought to get ahead in this business.

(She looks him over.)

You're pretty slick and handsome at that, ears and all. Good stage name, Pinocchio, isn't it?

*(*PINOCCHIO, *glum and morose, makes no answer.)*

My name is "The Peppermint Stick." Do you like it? Unusual name for a girl zebra. I'm glad to know you. We'll see a lot of each other. Cheer up, buddy! This isn't such a bad life. Always on the go, always doing something. And when you do your stuff good the public claps and yells and whistles and you feel like a million dollars.

(PINOCCHIO *is still silent.*)

Maybe you'll feel better tomorrow. Good night and sleep tight.

(She goes back to her stall and soon both little animals are asleep. The scene that follows is a mixture of dream and nightmare. First GEPPETTO *appears in a tiny sailboat, which may be cut out of cardboard.* GEPPETTO *stands behind it, holding it by the mast. He wanders aimlessly, tossing as if he were on the ocean.)*

GEPPETTO: Pinocchio! Pinocchio! Pinocchio!

*(*PINOCCHIO *wakes up, pricks his ears and, recognizing* GEPPETTO'S *voice, begins to weep.)*

PINOCCHIO: Dada!

GEPPETTO *(oblivious of Pinocchio's presence, continues to call)*: Pinocchio! Pinocchio! Pinocchio!

(Suddenly thunder is heard, the lights go out, and the boat disappears, apparently wrecked by the storm. Through the thunder GEPPETTO *is heard faintly calling.)*

Help! Help! Pinocchio! Help!

PINOCCHIO: Dada, dada!

(This futile response comes out donkey fashion. When the lights come on again there is no sign of GEPPETTO. *The* BLUE FAIRY *appears carrying a tray piled with good things to eat. Like* GEPPETTO *she wanders all over the scene looking and calling for* PINOCCHIO.)

BLUE FAIRY: Pinocchio! Pinocchio! Where can he be this time. Pinocchio! Your dinner has been waiting for you for five months now. Pretty soon it will all be cold. Pinocchio! Pinocchio!

PINOCCHIO *(He is choked with tears.)*: Maa! Maa! My Blue Fairy! Here I am! Maa! Maa!

BLUE FAIRY: What's that frightful noise? Oh, just a poor

donkey. I'm looking for Pinocchio, not you. Pinocchio! Pinocchio!

PINOCCHIO: It's me! I'm Pinocchio! Maa! Maa!

BLUE FAIRY: Where are you, Pinocchio? Pinocchio! Pinocchio!

(PINOCCHIO, *who is terrified, screams for help, which results in a string of loud ugly brayings.*)

ZEBRA *(waking up)*: You're worse than an alarm clock.

(The braying reaches the ears of TONY, *the groom, who enters to see what has happened. It is now morning.)*

TONY: Good morning, you healthy little fellow. A real early worm, aren't you? *(Seeing the empty box and bag.)* And you've already had breakfast too—and lunch too, you little rascal. Faker, that's what you are—a perfect faker. Come on now, little one. Let us begin to work.

(He pulls PINOCCHIO *to his feet and leads him around in a circle, making him go faster and faster.)*

Come on, come on! This will limber up your pins. Come on. Peppy, show Pinocchio how to do it.

*(*PEPPERMINT *runs around in beautiful circles for* PINOCCHIO'S *benefit. He tries hard to imitate her. The exercise is continued for a few minutes.* TONY *cracks his whip over them occasionally so that they do not lag.)*

TONY: All right. *(They stop.)* Up, Peppy. Show him how to stand up like a gentleman.

*(*PEPPERMINT *stands on her hind legs.*)

Down.

(She comes down on all fours.)

Up—down—up—down. Ready, Pinocchio, up!

*(*PINOCCHIO *makes an effort which is not very graceful.* TONY *helps him.)*

Higher. Higher. Good. Up—down—up—down.

*(The two animals are made to do this exercise about a
dozen times. The next exercise is more difficult. It consists
in walking upright on the hind legs.)*

Ready, Peppy, show Pinocchio how to walk like a
gentleman.

*(Peppy stands on her hind legs and walks in a circle.
Pinocchio looks on doubtfully.)*

Right. Up, Pinocchio, up!

(Pinocchio stands.)

Step now, come on!

*(Pinocchio tries to walk on his hind legs, but decides it
is easier to drop on all fours.)*

Try again. Up, up, up, up!

*(Pinocchio unwillingly tries it again, but drops very
quickly.)*

Come on now. You can do it. No faking, mind.

(He cracks his whip impatiently.)

Show him again, Peppy—up!

(Peppy repeats the demonstration.)

Nothing to it, Pinocchio. Up! Up!

(Pinocchio refuses even to stand.)

Up! Up! Up! Ears stopped up, Pinocchio? Let us clean
them. Up!

*(He lashes Pinocchio's ears with his whip. Pinocchio
brays from the pain.)*

Up, up little faker. Up, up, up, up!

*(He lashes Pinocchio repeatedly until he finally obeys
to save himself from the stinging whip.)*

Fine! Now, stay like that and walk. Come, Peppy, lead
him!

*(Peppermint leads the circular promenade. With every
two or three steps Pinocchio drops on all fours, only to be
whipped into an upright position again by Tony's ready and*

vicious whip. When they have made a circle three or four times they are allowed to relax.)

TONY: All right! Very good, Pinocchio. Only not so much cheating. Watch this little girl here. She's a fine model. Aren't you, Peppermint Stick?

(He pats them both affectionately.)

Now let us run around again while we rest. All right. Go!

(He snaps his whip, which starts PEPPERMINT *running in a circle again, with* PINOCCHIO *following.)*

Ready now, Peppy, skip.

(He snaps his whip, and PEPPERMINT *falls into a jumping step which looks like a chain of hurdle jumps.* PINOCCHIO *does not take the cue, but continues to run casually until he receives a sharp whack on the hind quarters. Like magic he immediately can jump along the* PEPPERMINT *way. Whenever he cheats, and he does so quite often, the whip puts him right.)*

That's right, Pinocchio. Keep your mind on it. Jump, jump, jump! Excellent! Very promising! Elegant! Nothing less! All right. Get ready for the hoop! Peppy! Run!

(They run around in a circle again at a faster pace than before. Then TONY, *with a large red hoop in his hand, takes a position at one point of the circle so that the animals can leap through it.)*

TONY: Jump!

(He holds out the hoop, cracks the whip, and PEPPERMINT *takes a neat leap which clears the hoop. When* PINOCCHIO'S *turn comes he stops in front of the hoop very much frightened. Then he goes around it.)*

TONY: Oh no, Pinocchio, that's the wrong hole. All right, Peppy, show him again. Jump!

*(*PEPPERMINT *repeats the leap through the hoop, but* PINOCCHIO *still remains stubborn. He stops at the hoop again, brays and goes around it. This time he gets the whip.)*

Once more, Peppy, darling—we have a hard egg.

(PEPPERMINT *goes through the hoop.*)

Now, Pinocchio, jump, jump!

(Again PINOCCHIO *stops in front of the hoop and brays loudly. This time he sounds ludicrously like a bawling child.)*

Jump! Jump! Shame on you, Pinocchio!

(He plants his boot on PINOCCHIO's *rump, but* PINOC-CHIO *only bawls louder and then, struck with an idea, he falls in a heap on the floor and moans like a very sick donkey.* TONY, *much amused, shakes his head and contemplates the prostrate* PINOCCHIO, *chuckling to himself. In the meantime,* MR. BILLY, *who has heard the braying, comes on the scene to see what it is all about.)*

MR. BILLY: What's the noise? What's the big horn about? Is that Pinocchio on the floor? Is he dead already? That promising future star already gone to join the heavenly ones?

TONY *(winking at* MR. BILLY): No, but I think he is dying, Bill. Shame. An awfully good specimen for a donkey.

MR. BILLY: What's the matter? Heart?

TONY: Combination of heart, liver, and spleen, I think.

MR. BILLY: Let me see, let me see.

(He kneels over PINOCCHIO, *puts his ear to his ribs and taps him all over with his whip handle.)*

Not serious. Overheated around the head. We'll fix him all right. *(He calls.)* Oh, Bones! Bring me a pail of ice water. Put plenty of ice in it. *(To* TONY.) If that doesn't do, we'll try something else *(significantly shaking his whip)* something hot. How's Peppermint this morning? You don't get hot in the head, do you, sweetheart?

*(*PEPPERMINT *rubs her nose against him.* BONES, *a Negro porter dressed in overalls, brings in a bucket of ice water.)*

That's right, Bones. See that handsome little donkey

down there? Poor thing was overcome by heat. Just cool
him off with that ice water. Got plenty of ice in it?

BONES: Sure has, boss.

BILLY: All right. Let him have it, Bones.

(PINOCCHIO *raises his head and sees* BONES *getting ready
to pour the water over him. He leaps to his feet and bolts off
the scene, braying dreadfully, to the delight of the circus
people, who laugh and laugh.*)

A jewel!

(*They are still laughing when the curtain falls.*)

SCENE TWO. *The first part of the scene takes place in front
of the curtain before it rises. The booming of a bass drum is
heard off-stage. Two clowns then appear. One is carrying a
large poster nailed to a pole. He also supports a large bass
drum on his back, which the other clown beats ferociously
as they walk back and forth across the stage. The poster reads:*

"Billy's Circus

Biggest One-Ring Circus on Earth

Special Feature

Beginning Today

The Celebrated Donkey, PINOCCHIO

Acclaimed the Star of the Ballerinos."

CLOWN (*who beats the drum repeats from time to time like
a parrot*): Billy's circus is illuminated with extra special
daylight illumination. All the other wonders, acrobats,
clowns, animal acts, and races will perform as usual.

BILLY: And now, ladies and gentlemen, I have the unusual,
unique pleasure of presenting to you the super-feature of
the program. Furthermore, no circus is so fortunate as to
be able to boast of one super-feature of all time. Estimable
ladies and gentlemen, you have the good fortune to witness

one of these rare and precious performances. I give you our special super-feature—THE GREAT PINOCCHIO! Otherwise known as the Donkey Star.

(About this time the BLUE FAIRY *walks across the stage, apparently no one notices her. The* RINGMASTER *cracks his whip, at which* PINOCCHIO *prances in. He is decorated and trimmed with silk tasseled trappings and brass bells. His tail is tied with a bow, his white enameled hoofs are edged with gold and his ears are covered with red silk upholstery, gold tasseled at the point. His entrance is greeted with loud applause.)*

BILLY: Ladies and gentlemen, the renowned Pinocchio. Observe him, to all appearances a mild handsome donkey. In actuality as wild a specimen as the leopard. Trapped and extricated from the precipices of Borneo—my efforts to domesticate him have been futile. Mark well his wild, restless eyes, only a small inkling to his incredible temper. Notice, however, this peculiar bump on his forehead. That, ladies and gentlemen, is the source and fountain of his genius. It is the unmistakable bump which is the distinguished birthmark of all great dancers—beast as well as man. Pinocchio has had the honor to perform before all the important crowned heads of Europe and before two ex-presidents of the United States. And now, ladies and gentlemen, I leave you to judge this animal for yourselves.

(He turns to PINOCCHIO, *snapping his whip.)*

Bow, Pinocchio! Greet these ladies, gentlemen and your faithful little friends. Bow!

*(*PINOCCHIO *goes down on his front knees and inclines and raises his head several times. The spectators applaud. At the snap of the whip* PINOCCHIO *rises.)*

Show us how gentlemen promenade in the park, Pinocchio.

(He snaps his whip and PINOCCHIO *walks with an elegant high step around the ring, holding his head very high.)*

Show us how the stars at the royal theatre walk, Pinocchio.

*(*PINOCCHIO *stands on his hind legs, takes a large cane which the* RINGMASTER *hands him in his front paws, and walks around the ring swinging the cane. Next the* RINGMASTER *cracks his whip and* PINOCCHIO *starts to pace around the ring. With every other crack of the whip he accelerates his pace until he is galloping around the ring at a great speed. Suddenly the* RINGMASTER *shoots off a pistol and* PINOCCHIO *falls to the ground as if shot dead. The spectators applaud enthusiastically and yell: "Bravo." A familiar sound reaches* PINOCCHIO'S *long ears in those bravos. He raises his head and looks in the direction of the* BLUE FAIRY. *He stares and stares; then, slowly rising, he approaches her. The face of the* BLUE FAIRY *makes* PINOCCHIO *forget that he is the star of the circus and he breaks out into loud doleful brayings. He tries to say the* BLUE FAIRY'S *name but he only succeeds in braying out: Ma— a—a—a—a! M—a—a—a!" The spectators go into fits of laughter at the bit of unexpected farce on* PINOCCHIO'S *part. The* RINGMASTER *finally goes after* PINOCCHIO *and drags him back to the center of the ring. The* BLUE FAIRY *quickly disappears and is seen no more.)*

BILLY: Before we go on to the dance exhibition Pinocchio will accommodate us with some of his accomplished high jumps through the hoop.

(Two circus hands stand on stools and hold a large gold and red hoop between them above their heads.)

Ladies and gentlemen, an unheard of feat for a donkey! Ready, Pinocchio, up!

*(*PINOCCHIO, *whose mind is no longer on his performance, runs under the hoop and dashes to the spot where the* BLUE

FAIRY *sat. Not finding her he emits some mournful brays. The spectators enjoy* PINOCCHIO's *behavior immensely. The* RINGMASTER *brings him back and makes him try again. Again he runs under the hoop. Much disgusted, the* RINGMASTER *orders the two circus hands to come down off the stools and try holding the hoop lower at first.)*

BILLY: Come on now, Pinocchio. That's not too high for you. Come on! Begin with that! Up! Up!

(He cracks his whip impatiently over PINOCCHIO. PINOCCHIO *finally makes a leap through the hoop but his hind feet catch and he falls in a heap on the floor. The spectators laugh heartily and applaud. The* RINGMASTER, *furious, cracks his whip for* PINOCCHIO *to get up, but as the donkey doesn't move he lets him have a wicked blow on the back.* PINOCCHIO *moans, tries to get up, but collapses again. There is a short silence as though all had sensed an accident. The* RINGMASTER *kneels over* PINOCCHIO *and discovers that he has broken one of his forelegs. He rises.)*

Ladies and gentlemen, I am sorry to announce that the performance must be concluded abruptly. The poor animal's foreleg is broken and he is unable to stand. I regret, ladies and gentlemen, to have to say good night.

(The spectators make many sympathetic remarks and end by applauding and cheering and yelling: "Bravo, Pinocchio!" The RINGMASTER *bows graciously many times. Slowly the people go, leaving* PINOCCHIO *in the hands of his masters.)*

BILLY: Call the doctor.

(One of the circus hands goes out. BILLY *examines* PINOCCHIO's *leg.)*

Some funny devil got into you tonight, Pinocchio. You haven't carried on like that since I first bought you. Just had to spoil the whole show—and maybe for good, too. You're a bad egg but I guess we'll forgive you.

(The circus DOCTOR *enters.)*

DOCTOR: What's up, chief? Is it bad?

BILLY: Don't know, doc. I think his leg is broken. Take a look.

(The DOCTOR *examines* PINOCCHIO'S *leg carefully. He doesn't say anything for some time, but shakes his head now and then.)*

DOCTOR: I guess he's done it. Feels to me like a break that won't heal for months and maybe years. One thing is certain: his career is over. He'll never be able to do his stuff again.

BILLY: What? Never?

DOCTOR: That's my candid opinion. In fact, you would be fooling yourself to hold out any hope that he'll ever be anything but a lame donkey.

BILLY: Wow!

(He paces the ring silently for a few moments. All wait for his decision very silently. He suddenly flings his whip on the floor and speaks with ill disguised grief.)

Shoot him and give his carcass to the lions.

CIRCUS HAND: Don't shoot him, Mr. Billy. The band needs a fine new bass drum. That hide of his ought to make a fine drum head. Drown him first, then we can take his skin and give the rest to the lions.

BILLY: Fine! Hey there, Bones!

BONES: Yessuh!

BILLY: Take this lame donkey to the river, tie a rope around his neck, and throw him in. When he's drowned, pull him out and leave him on the rocks. We're going to make a new drum.

BONES: Yessuh, boss! Come along, Pinocchio.

(The fancy paraphernalia is all stripped off PINOCCHIO, *a rope is tied around his neck and he is led limping off the*

scene. BONES *sings something about "de ribber."* BILLY *and the others are a sad little group.* PINOCCHIO *has been quite a favorite and much loved. He has left four broken hearts in the circus ring. They haven't even dared to say good-by to him.*)

DOCTOR: Think that you will train another donkey, chief?

BILLY: Where will you find one? Donkeys don't come like that. Sometimes Pinocchio didn't act like a donkey at all. Funny beast—too human.

DOCTOR: If there was one, there must be others.

BILLY: Maybe. I have my doubts.

(*A long silence follows. Everyone is occupied with his own sad thoughts. Suddenly the silence is broken by the voice of a distressed Negro calling, "Boss! Boss!" Then* BONES *rushes in shaking all over.*)

BONES: He's a hant, boss! Dat donkey ain't no donkey, boss! He was habitated by de dibble.

BILLY: What's the matter, what's the matter, Bones?

BONES: Dat donkey am a dibble. He ain't no donkey.

BILLY: Where did you leave him? What did you do with him? What happened?

BONES: I pushed a donkey in de ribber, boss, but when I went to pull him out agin the rope was very light and when I looked it was catching de dibble by the neck.

BILLY: Come now, Bones, you're dreaming.

BONES: No suh, boss! That was sho de dibble came out ob de ribber!

BILLY: What kind of a devil was he? What did it look like?

BONES: He was very skinny and rattled like he was made of wood and he had a long nose dat stuck out like a horn. I'se scared, boss.

BILLY: What did you do with it?

BONES: I just dropped him back in de ribber, rope and all, and made tracks fast.

(They all laugh heartily.)

BILLY: Well, that's that. Let's say a few words to the memory of Pinocchio, the ex-star of the circus.

ALL: GOOD RIDDANCE!

(The curtain falls.)

SCENE THREE. *This scene represents the interior of the whale. A background of black or purple cloth with ropes hanging down from the top at various angles may be used effectively. Very little light should be used during this scene. Occasionally it may be lit up brightly for two or three seconds at a time by a strong light turned on and off in one of the wings so that it looks like sunlight coming through the open mouth of the whale, to be obscured again when the mouth closes. Strange grinding and whistling noises should be heard continuously. When the curtain rises a great gust of wind sweeps the scene (use an electric fan from one of the wings) and a moment later* PINOCCHIO *tumbles in. Flashes of light show* PINOCCHIO *crying all in a heap.*

PINOCCHIO: Help! Help me! Help! Help! Isn't there anybody who can help me. Poor Pinocchio! Poor me! Help!

(Through the darkness is heard a voice that sounds like a guitar very much out of tune.)

VOICE OF TUNNY: You poor unfortunate. What help do you expect to find here?

PINOCCHIO: Who is it? Who is talking?

VOICE OF TUNNY: It is I. Just a poor Tunny. I was swallowed by the whale along with you. What kind of a fish are you, anyway?

PINOCCHIO: I'm no kind of fish. I'm a puppet, a wooden puppet.

VOICE OF TUNNY: Why did you let this sea monster swallow you then, if you're not a fish.

PINOCCHIO: I didn't let him swallow me; he just swallowed me by himself. And now what are we going to do in this darkness?

VOICE OF TUNNEY: What are we going to do? I don't know. Get used to it.

PINOCCHIO: That's just what I don't want to do.

VOICE OF TUNNY: I don't either as far as that goes—but I'm a philosopher.

PINOCCHIO: Nonsense!

VOICE OF TUNNY: That's just my viewpoint. A viewpoint, among the politicians of my species, is respected.

PINOCCHIO: Well, I don't care. I want to get out of here. I want to escape.

VOICE OF TUNNY: Escape if you can and good luck to you.

PINOCCHIO: Is this whale very big?

VOICE OF TUNNY: His body, not including the tail, is a mile long. Judge for yourself. (PINOCCHIO *whistles. Then he perceives a faint light in the distance.*)

PINOCCHIO: What's that tiny light that looks like a blinking star way down there?

VOICE OF TUNNY: I don't know. Very likely somebody else.

PINOCCHIO: I'm going to visit him. Is there any old fish around anywhere who could show me how to escape from here?

VOICE OF TUNNY: Who knows? Good luck to you, brave puppet.

PINOCCHIO: Good-by, Mr. Tunny Fish.

VOICE OF TUNNY: Good-by and good luck again, brave puppet.

PINOCCHIO: When shall we meet again—and where?

VOICE OF TUNNY: Who knows? Better not think of it.

(The grinding and other noises become louder as Pinoc- chio *begins to walk in the direction of the light. As the light grows brighter it shows an old man with long white hair and a beard leaning sadly against the wall; the old man happens to be* Geppetto. *When* Pinocchio *sees the old man he stops in astonishment. He stares for a moment; then he bursts out.)*

Pinocchio: Dada! My dear, dear dada! It's you! I've found you at last. Oh my dada! I'll never leave you again, never, never!

Geppetto: Gracious! Goodness! Are my old eyes playing tricks on me? Is it true? Are you really my little Pinocchio?

Pinocchio: Of course it's me, dada! Your little Pinocchio!

(They dance in glee.)

Geppetto: It's really my little Pinocchio; all safe and sound— not even his hat is lost!

Pinocchio: You have long whiskers now, dada! But I would know you even if they were longer, and even if you painted your face black.

Geppetto: My little Pinocchio. Let me see. *(He looks him over, pulling his nose.)* You really are my Pinocchio, aren't you?

Pinocchio: Of course. Certainly. Positively.

Geppetto: How did you fall into this place?

Pinocchio: Oh, my dear dada, if you only knew all the awful things—since you sold your only coat to buy me a book and I ran away. How long have you been locked up in here?

Geppetto: Months and months. Ever since they let me out of jail. I heard you were off in a strange land so I built a little boat and went searching for you.

Pinocchio: And how did you keep alive? Where did you get the candle? And the matches? And everything?

Geppetto: That was the strange luck of it. It just happened that the very same storm that wrecked my boat also wrecked a merchant ship not far away. The sailors were saved, but as the ship sank, this whale of ours, thanks to his excellent appetite, swallowed her just as she was.

PINOCCHIO: All at once, in one bite?

GEPPETTO: In one bite. The ship was loaded with all kinds of canned food, biscuits, wine in bottles and barrels, raisins, cheese, chocolate, coffee, condensed milk, sugar, candles and safety matches. This grand gift of Providence has kept me alive all this time. But my provisions have just run out today. This is the last candle, which I lit with the last match.

PINOCCHIO: And after that?

GEPPETTO: After that, Pinocchio, we shall be left in the dark.

PINOCCHIO: Gee! In that case, there's no time to lose, dada. We must escape right away.

GEPPETTO: Escape? How and where?

PINOCCHIO: By climbing out of his mouth and swimming away.

GEPPETTO: That's a good idea, no doubt, if I only could swim, but I can't.

PINOCCHIO: That's nothing. I'm a good swimmer because I can't sink. You can get on my back and then I'll swim to the shore.

GEPPETTO: It's not so easy, child! You forget that you're so little and I so big.

PINOCCHIO: You'll see! I'll show you! Come on, dada, you follow me and don't be afraid.

(*He takes the candle and leads the way.*)

Look, dada, look! That must be his mouth.

GEPPETTO: It's nice and open because the poor monster has asthma. Feel the wind from his lungs. Careful it doesn't blow out the candle.

PINOCCHIO: Wait here a minute, dada. Let me see if it's all right.

(He leaves Geppetto *in the darkness and goes off the scene for a moment to investigate. He returns well satisfied.)*

There's a full moon out too. It's just right to escape. The whale is sound asleep, so let's hurry up. The water is very calm too. Give me your hand, dada. In five minutes we'll be swimming away safely. Come on. His throat is just like a stepladder.

(Hand in hand they slowly go off the scene, walking on tiptoes. A few moments of silence follow except for the audible breathing of the asthmatic monster and the faint grinding of his complicated machinery. All of a sudden a terrific noise is heard which sounds like a sneeze coming through a gigantic amplifier. It may be produced by violently waving a long sheet of thin metal and ending up with the clashing of cymbals. At the same time Pinocchio *and* Geppetto *are hurled back on the scene without the candle. There is total darkness. They are both very much frightened.)*

Pinocchio: Dada!

Geppetto: Pinocchio!

Pinocchio: Where are you?

Geppetto: I'm here. Where are you?

Pinocchio: Here. The candle went out. What happened?

Geppetto: I think anything would have gone out. I think the whale sneezed. We must have tickled him somehow.

Pinocchio: Yeah. Haven't you got even one more match?

Geppetto: Not one. I'm afraid we're lost now, son.

Pinocchio: Not yet. We don't need a candle anyway. Look, look! The mouth is opening again. There's the moon! Come on, dada!

Geppetto: Where are you going, Pinocchio?

Pinocchio: We must try again. Let us walk more to one side.

Geppetto: You're a brave little hero, Pinocchio. But I'm afraid I had better stay behind.

PINOCCHIO: Come on. It's easy.

GEPPETTO: You'll sink with my weight, Pinocchio.

PINOCCHIO: No, I won't. I'll prove it.

GEPPETTO: Pinocchio, we'll both drown.

PINOCCHIO: It's better than being eaten, isn't it?

GEPPETTO: You go and let me stay.

PINOCCHIO: No, no, no, no! I'm a swell swimmer and I'll show you that I can carry you on my back.

GEPPETTO: I didn't see any land in sight. All I saw was sky, sky, sky—water, water, water.

PINOCCHIO: But I saw land too—lots of it. I didn't tell you that I'm like a cat. My eyes see better in the night time than in the day.

GEPPETTO: We shall both drown. I'm sure we shall both drown, Pinocchio.

VOICE OF TUNNY: Who will drown? Why do you want to drown? Don't you like to live?

GEPPETTO: We both like to live very much but I'm afraid that we are both going to drown—Pinocchio and I.

VOICE OF TUNNY: Hello, Pinocchio. You're the wooden puppet, aren't you?

PINOCCHIO: Uh huh. And are you the tunny fish that I thought was a guitar?

VOICE OF TUNNY: That's right—in the cellar of the whale.

PINOCCHIO (*looking up*): How did you get out?

VOICE OF TUNNY: I followed your example. Why did you go back? I watched you come up and followed you. I'm a free tunny again and going to visit my family, who must be wondering where I am—all my little tunnies.

PINOCCHIO: Would you do me and my father a favor first, good Tunny?

VOICE OF TUNNY: If it's easy. What is it?

PINOCCHIO: I can swim but my dada can't and if I carry him

on my back, then maybe we'll both get drowned and we
want to reach land before we drown because I want to see
the Blue Fairy, who is my mother. So if you'll let us get
on your back, we'll be glad. Won't we?

GEPPETTO: And very grateful.

VOICE OF TUNNY: Is that all? That's easy. Come out and get
on—both of you.

PINOCCHIO: Come on, dada. We're coming.

*(Both GEPPETTO and PINOCCHIO go off the scene quickly
and the rest of the scene is heard through the open mouth.)*
Are we heavy?

VOICE OF TUNNY: Heavy? Are you on already?

PINOCCHIO: Yes. We're both on and ready.

VOICE OF TUNNY: You must be made of shadows. Haven't you
got any baggage?

PINOCCHIO: No. Just us.

VOICE OF TUNNY: All right. Get ready and hold tight. You'll
find any number of loose fins around. Let's go!

PINOCCHIO: Hurray! Hurray! Hurray!

*(The voices die off in the distance. The lights go out
and a plain blue drop is lowered in front of that used in the
first part of the scene. Some cardboard cut-outs painted to
look like rocks can be placed around. When the change is
made the lights come on again. PINOCCHIO jumps on the scene
from behind the rocks, followed by GEPPETTO.)*
Hurray! Hurray! And here we are! Hurray, hurray, hurray!

VOICE OF TUNNY *(who is completely hidden behind the rocks)*:
Gracious! For your weight you can make a gigantic lot of
noise.

PINOCCHIO: Come on, dada! This is the land. Land! And you
won't sink on it. My dear Tunny Fish, you have saved my
dada's life and I don't know how to thank you because I
would never be able to thank you enough.

VOICE OF TUNNY: Oh, that's nothing, Pinocchio. It was very easy.

PINOCCHIO: Let me at least give you a kiss as a sign of my gratitude, and so I'll never forget you.

(PINOCCHIO *kneels down and kisses the invisible tunny fish.*)

VOICE OF TUNNY: Well, good-by and good luck. If ever you're visiting in the ocean again, come and see me.

PINOCCHIO: Good-by, kind Tunny; regards to all the little tunnies.

GEPPETTO: Good-by.

(*They both wave the tunny good-by for a long time until he is quite out of sight.*)

PINOCCHIO: Hurray, hurray, hurray! Here we are, dada! Now let us go.

GEPPETTO: Now that we are here, where can we go?

(*He looks about helplessly.*)

PINOCCHIO: We'll go somewhere and then we'll get something to eat and then we'll find a place to sleep. See that little white house with a red roof?

(GEPPETTO *looks where* PINOCCHIO *is pointing but gives no indication that he sees the house.*)

Maybe it's too far for you to see it. Let us go that way. Maybe it's a village.

(*They reach the house and look in.*)

PINOCCHIO: Is there anything to eat?

GEPPETTO: Not much! We'll have to work for our food.

PINOCCHIO: Hurray! I'll work from morning until night, every day, and buy my dada everything he needs. Let us hurry up and go into the house.

(*The curtain falls.*)

SCENE FOUR. *This final scene represents the interior of the little red and white cottage where* PINOCCHIO *and* GEPPETTO *have taken up their abode. A bed, a stool and a picture of the* BLUE FAIRY, *drawn from* PINOCCHIO'S *memory, are the furnishings of the room. The moon may be seen through the window, throwing a faint light in the room.* PINOCCHIO *is in bed sound asleep. The night appears to be like an ordinary night which children fill with sleep. But suddenly this turns into an eventful night for this little red and white cottage. A few moments after the curtain rises, the stillness is broken by the tinkling of bells in the distance, which grow louder and louder. Finally when the bells have become so loud and confused that they are almost deafening they stop altogether as if obeying the baton of a conductor. The* BLUE FAIRY'S *coach, drawn by goodness knows how many horses, has come to a halt outside the door. Presently the door opens, apparently all by itself, and one by one in file any number of dogs, dressed in the red livery of the* BLUE FAIRY'S *household. Each dog carries a lantern. They lift the bed and carry it to the center of the scene the better to perform the ceremony which is about to follow. There must be at least enough dogs to make a complete circle around the bed. They run around the bed first one way, then the other, emitting gay little barks all the while which sound like perfectly good tunes if one happens to understand dog language. When they have finished their little song and dance they remain standing in a circle around the bed and hold the lanterns high above their heads, to throw light on* PINOCCHIO. *A drum begins to beat outside the house which sounds something like the tom-tom of an African ceremonial dance. This announces the entrance of the* BLUE FAIRY. *She is dressed in a beautiful blue silk cloak spattered with silver stars which trails several feet behind her. At the back of her head is a huge silver star standing high like a Spanish comb, except that this looks like a halo. In her hand she has a scepter, which is filled with the water of life. The dogs make a wide circle so that the* BLUE FAIRY *can easily*

move around inside it. As she chants the following incanta-
tion she goes through a delicate dance around the sleeping
PINOCCHIO, *sprinkling the water of life over him at the end*
of each phrase.

BLUE FAIRY: Pinocchio of wood, of ordinary wood,
        Have you been bad or have you been good?

PINOCCHIO *(in his sleep as he answers all the questions that*
  follow): Sometimes bad and sometimes good.

BLUE FAIRY: Let us weigh the night and the day,
        Which is heavier, grass or hay?

CHORUS OF DOGS:
        One is one and two is two,
        Two and one make magic three,
        One, two, three will set him free
        From wood that is bad
        And wood that is good.

BLUE FAIRY: Have you thirsted, Pinocchio?
PINOCCHIO: Yes.
BLUE FAIRY: Have you hungered, Pinocchio?
PINOCCHIO: Yes.
BLUE FAIRY: Have you wept, Pinocchio?
PINOCCHIO: Yes.
BLUE FAIRY: Have you laughed, Pinocchio?
PINOCCHIO: Yes.
BLUE FAIRY: Have you disobeyed, Pinocchio?
PINOCCHIO: Yes.
BLUE FAIRY: Have you lied, Pinocchio?
PINOCCHIO: Yes.
BLUE FAIRY: Have you grieved, Pinocchio?
PINOCCHIO: Yes, yes.
BLUE FAIRY: Have you repented, Pinocchio?
PINOCCHIO: Yes, yes.
BLUE FAIRY: How, Pinocchio, how?

PINOCCHIO: Go to school—study—arithmetic—spelling—
reading—take—care—of—dada.

*(As she chants the following words the dogs circle around
the bed in one direction still holding the lanterns aloft and
barking, while she circles in the other direction.)*

BLUE FAIRY: Weigh the good against the bad
        And you have what should be had.
        Puppet made of nails and wood,
        Be a lad handsome and good.
        Hair of paint, be real and thick,
        Eyes of glass, be blue and quick,
        Nose, be smaller than you are,
        Mouth, be like a rising star,
        Hands, be dexterous and strong,
        Feet, keep him from walking wrong.
        Let us fashion him a heart
        That will sing like the lark,
        And concoct for him a brain
        That will work in sun and rain.
        Sleep, sleep, and when you wake
        Be this dear lad for my sake.

*(A rooster is heard crowing, which is the herald that
warns all magic to cease. The* BLUE FAIRY *sweeps out of the
door followed by her long starry train and the chorus of dogs.
A moment later the deafening jingle of the horse bells is
heard, and before it completely dies out in the distance, the
curtain falls for a very short space of time. No change is made
in the scenery except that a wooden figure of* PINOCCHIO *is
either placed on a chair or suspended from the ceiling at the
foot of the bed so that, on awakening,* PINOCCHIO *will immediately see his former self. If it is found preferable not to
lower the curtain, the wooden figure should then be arranged
in place during the ceremony. The curtain should rise again*

almost immediately when the bells stop jingling. It is no longer night but bright morning. The new PINOCCHIO *is still sleeping peacefully. Needless to say, he no longer resembles a wooden puppet in any way. He is just a handsome little boy. You can use another, better-looking puppet, for the new puppet. A knock is heard at the door. It is a neighbor for whom* PINOCCHIO *has been doing odd jobs in exchange for milk for* GEPPETTO.)

NEIGHBOR: Pinocchio! Pinocchio! *(He opens a door and puts the glass of milk on the stool without glancing at* PINOC-CHIO.) There, Pinocchio, here's the milk for your old Daddy, Geppetto. All the trouble in the world comes to me. What a calamity, what a calamity! Now my jackass is deciding to die on me. It's terrible, it's terrible! I'll need more help now. Maybe you can earn two glasses of milk a day, Pinocchio. Then you can drink one yourself and maybe you'll get some color in your cheeks. What a life, what a life! Why do donkeys have to get sick and die on poor men? Get up, Pinocchio, get up, get up!

(PINOCCHIO *wakes up and stares about him very much dazed.)*

PINOCCHIO: What time is it?

NEIGHBOR: What time? Very high time. I've milked seven goats and taken them to the mountains and delivered my milk, even yours, and brought home a fool donkey that has made up its mind to die on me before it reaches the stable. What a life, what a life—and some people can sleep! *(He goes off still muttering to himself.* PINOCCHIO's *bewilderment increases. He looks at his hands for a long time, turning them over and over.)*

PINOCCHIO: Real hands! *(He kicks up his feet and feels them.)* Real feet. *(He takes his face in his hands.)* Real. *(He pinches his arm.)* Ouch! Real! Everything! I wonder if I'm dreaming. I wish I never woke up. *(For the first time he discovers the limp wooden* PINOCCHIO *hanging near the foot of the bed.)* Hey, Pinocchio, aren't you Pinocchio? *(He gets out of the bed and approaches the wooden puppet cautiously. His elegant pajamas, the* BLUE FAIRY'S *gift, momentarily break his train of thought, but his mind finally goes back to the wooden* PINOCCHIO.*)* Hey! Pinocchio! Aren't you Pinocchio? What's the matter? *(As he addresses the puppet, it evinces no sign of life.)* I must be Pinocchio! Am I Pinocchio or are you? I must be Pinocchio because I feel like Pinocchio used to. *(He perceives a large beautifully framed hand mirror which the* BLUE FAIRY *has left there for a good reason. He picks it up and looks in it. The sight so fascinates him that his eyes remain glued to it for the longest time. He chuckles and feels his face, particularly his nose, which he compares with the wooden* PINOCCHIO's *long nose, and is on the whole tremendously pleased with his reflected self. He suddenly remembers* GEPPETTO *and starts calling.)* Dada! Dada! *(He dashes into an adjoining room still calling.)* Dada! where are you? Dada! *(He comes back looking very sad, on the verge of tears.)* I knew I was dreaming, I'll never be a real boy for real, just in dreams. *(He begins to cry on his former self's shoulder.)* You're just fooling me. When it's tomorrow, you'll jump around again like always, and I'll always be made of wood. Oh, my Blue Fairy Mother, why don't you come to see me when I'm not just dreaming? *(Without a warning, a loud jingling of bells is heard outside the door, which again ends abruptly, and the* BLUE FAIRY *in her flowing mantle enters.)*

BLUE FAIRY: Good morning, Pinocchio dear. Come greet your mother. How did you know I was coming?

PINOCCHIO *(He rushes to embrace her.)*: My Blue Fairy Mother! My Blue Fairy! But I'm only dreaming. I know it.

I'm sure of it! Because there's Pinocchio over there and he's fooling me too because he won't talk or move.

BLUE FAIRY: That's not Pinocchio, dear. That was Pinocchio and you are Pinocchio. But what a change!

PINOCCHIO: If I'm not dreaming, where's my dada? My dada, Geppetto? He's not well and he's not in his bed.

BLUE FAIRY: Oh, don't you know? Geppetto is very well now too. He got up at sunrise and went to the town to buy himself some good lumber.

PINOCCHIO: What?

BLUE FAIRY: Oh, he is going to carve some nice furniture and things for you. (GEPPETTO *enters hale and hearty, looking very much as he did when he started to carve* PINOCCHIO. *He is carrying a beautiful piece of lumber.* PINOCCHIO *runs to him and throws his arms around his neck.*)

PINOCCHIO: Dada! Do you know me? Am I really me?

GEPPETTO: Well, well, my little Pinocchio! Of course it's you—just as you as I am I. Good morning, beautiful Blue Fairy. I see you have changed my little wooden effort into a handsome smart lad. *(He compares the wooden* PINOCCHIO *with the living one, laughing gayly.)* There is a little difference between these two individuals. And to think that once upon a time this was the terrible imp it was.

BLUE FAIRY: There were more good qualities in it than bad, Geppetto, otherwise the result might have been quite different.

PINOCCHIO: Hurry, hurry, hurry.

BLUE FAIRY: And now my little handsome, obedient Pinocchio, we will celebrate this thrilling event, as I promised we would.

(She claps her hands, which is a signal for the dogs in red livery to bring in a very long narrow table all set with many good things to eat. There are two or three dozen places

arranged. The dogs remove the bed and place the table in the center of the room. Little stools are placed around it to be occupied by many little visitors not yet there. PINOCCHIO *is thrilled beyond words. All he can do is chuckle excitedly as he discovers one thing after another and bursts forth with ejaculations. Finally three black dogs dressed in evening clothes come in, bow and sit at one end of the room. One has a drum, one an accordion and the other cymbals.)*

BLUE FAIRY: All your little friends have been invited, Pinocchio. They are all waiting outside. Will you ask them in?

PINOCCHIO: Outside? Where? *(He runs outside, and a moment later a score of little voices are heard cheering.* PINOCCHIO *leads the crowd of children inside. Among them are as many of the puppets as possible who have appeared in* PINOCCHIO'S *various adventures. As they are arranged at the table there is a continuous ripple of chatter and laughter and cheering. Everybody is wearing a fancy paper hat.)*

ONE OF THE GUESTS: Let us put the wood Pinocchio on the table! Yes, yes. Hooray for Pinocchio!

(Suddenly the NEIGHBOR *comes in, very much upset.)*

NEIGHBOR: Pinocchio! Where is Pinocchio? I'm waiting for you. Why don't you come over and do your work?

PINOCCHIO: Oh, I forgot.

BLUE FAIRY: This is Pinocchio's birthday, good neighbor. He musn't work today. He will start again tomorrow.

NEIGHBOR: But I need help—and my poor donkey is dying. Why do fool donkeys have to go and die when there's work to be done?

PINOCCHIO: Let me see what's the matter with him. I was—I mean I know something about donkeys, after all. I'll be right back.

(He goes out with the NEIGHBOR. *In a few minutes* PINOCCHIO *returns supporting a very sick donkey.)*

ALL THE GUESTS: Ah!

PINOCCHIO (*to the* BLUE FAIRY): May I invite this donkey to
my party, because this is Wick, an old friend of mine?

BLUE FAIRY: Of course, Pinocchio, of course! Help him in.
You join us too, good neighbor.

(*Some of the guests help* WICK, *the donkey, to the table
and give him a very prominent seat. The music and dancing
redouble. They all take hands and dance around the table as
the curtain falls.*)